*Season
of the
Butterfly*

Season of the Butterfly

Betty Donaldson

Troy Publishing

© Betty Donaldson

No part of this book may be reproduced or transmitted in any way or by any means, electronic or mechanical, including photocopying, recording, or any information storage and retrieval system, known to be invented, without permission in writing from the author. All rights reserved.

Published by:
Troy Publishing,
P.O. Box 46, Oxford   OX2 6DX

Typeset and Marketed by:
Summerfield Press,
Jane Geddes, 18 Summerfield, Oxford   OX1 4RU

Printed by:
Antony Rowe Ltd.
Bumper's Farm, Chippenham

ISBN: 0 9522435 04

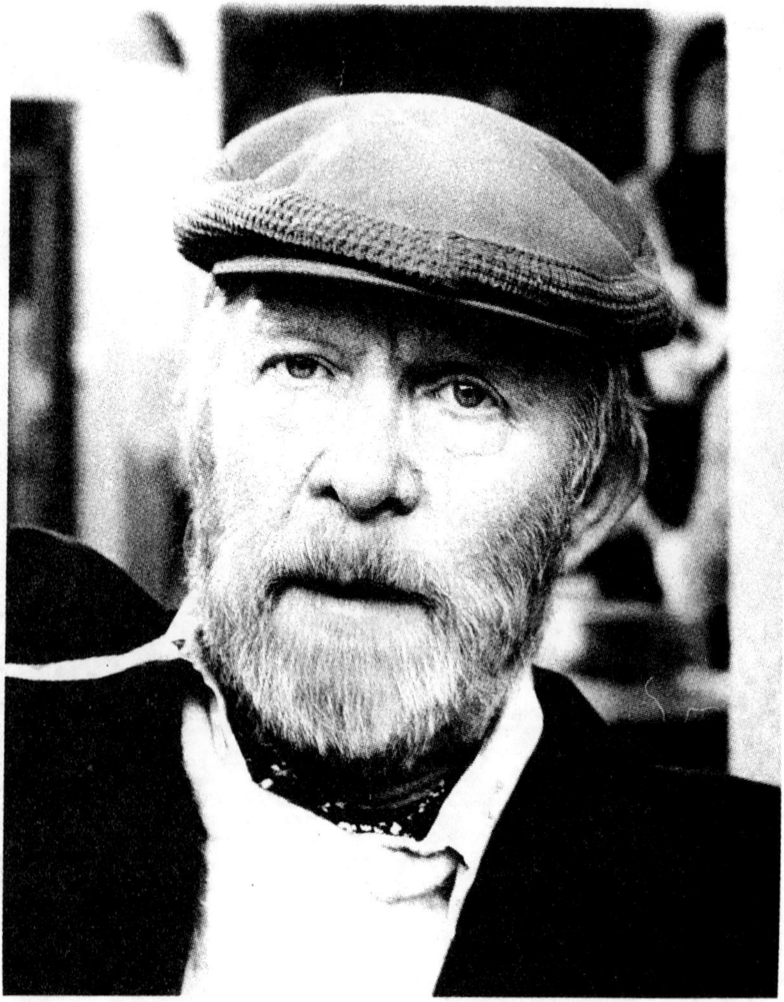

In memory of Jon

The never daunted trier and mentor, friend and husband

One shaft of sunlight to a captive brought
All problems of an enraged sun to naught.
Cupped trembling hands these minute prisms held,
This union with the living air
Is more than counted years not breathed before.
If chosen, sight and feeling can survive
Transforming time and place, each day alive.

Aged 19. From a Polish Dungeon

1920 - 1989

About the Author

Formed into a conventional and puritanical mode of thinking by boarding school education which began at the early age of five, Betty rejoined her parents in India at the age of sixteen and spent the war years heavily involved with the Burma War.

Betty was married and widowed within the year, her upbringing not allowing her to mourn freely. Marriage to another soldier who turned to the priesthood led her to another conventional lifestyle, with which she could not come to terms and was eventually forced to abandon.

Meeting with the free thinking Jon completed her emancipation and led to the writing of this book.

Season of the Butterfly

Story of an Extraordinary Dosser

Contents

Page No.

Prologue   *10*

Part One
CHAPTER ONE	Outside Apprenticeship	14
CHAPTER TWO	Working and Talking	26
CHAPTER THREE	Unscheduled Journey	39
CHAPTER FOUR	Here, There and Everywhere	50
CHAPTER FIVE	Colder and Colder	64

Part Two
CHAPTER SIX	The Assault	82
CHAPTER SEVEN	Gaol Bird	96
CHAPTER EIGHT	Knightsbridge	111
CHAPTER NINE	Dismissal and Dosser Arthur	122
CHAPTER TEN	Movements in Summertime	133

Part Three
CHAPTER ELEVEN	The Attack	150
CHAPTER TWELVE	Bereft	167
CHAPTER THIRTEEN	The Proposition	177
CHAPTER FOURTEEN	The Ace of Spades	187

Prologue

This is the story of part of the life of Jon Inglis, a most remarkable person, whose first twenty five years of hardship did not quell his search for truth, his love for people, and his need to think creatively and share his thoughts with his fellow man.

Born to a widow who supported her family by prostitution, he was packed off to the loveless environment of an orphanage. After ten years of rigid discipline and little food, he left and joined a travelling boxing booth. At the outbreak of the Second World War he joined the army. Soon he was sent to France where he dug ditches and drains and courted the French girls. When the British forces retreated before the German army, Jon was captured and taken prisoner. He was just eighteen. He had five years of harsh treatment in the German POW camps, suffering severely from the extra punishments meted out after escaping six times. At the end of the war he was returned to Germany as an Intelligence Officer, and during this time he met and married a German girl. He returned to England, settled in Weybridge and raised a family as well as founding a highly successful and profitable business.

Through all these years of hassle, tension and physical hardship, Jon managed to write poetry and prose. As he grew older he became more and more disillusioned with the competitiveness of commerce and he began to find that his philosophies led him further away from the conventions of family and business life: eventually he turned his back on all that his life had for him and took to the London streets as a dosser.

This story deals with this period giving a unique glimpse into the lifestyle and thought processes that being a dosser entailed. It also explains the daemon that drove Jon to make such a change, a daemon that made him search for the real meanings of life, to find values based on truth, and to allow his God, the Supreme Intelligence, to guide him. He sought to make a social change in current attitudes for he felt that chaos was not far away.

After years of hunger, fatigue, confrontations with the police, a physical attack and much communication with his fellow dosser, he emerged with his integrity intact. The unexpected happened in his third year. He found he loved a woman, deeply and passionately, and he had to make a choice, to go to his beloved or continue with his searchings and his quest for change.

Synopsis

or *A Liveable Option*

Within these timeless fields prevails an awe,
Of form and function's knowing law,
A tribute to the hereafter of herebefore,
Beholden within the now of evermore,
Bound in the answers of an unquestioning earth
Yielding, through change, an every giving girth
As transient kingdoms come to pass
To fall disarmed beneath unfailing grass.
Life's infinite and timely hand
Proffers supply to meet demand
Boundlessly, divining what 'need' must know
to ensure survival and awareness show,
And making belief, like the first smile, a cosmic glance
Persuasive in promise, leaving too much to chance.
For, galaxies beyond dogma's arresting role
Intelligence emerges unbetrayable in soul.

Time does remain free of fear
To go right back to the year
Truth alone inspired,
Then without stress, or mis-use of force,
To alter collision's course.
Time does remain to defuse the loss of gain
Exploited to the point of crime,
Yesterday's mis-use of time.

Part One

CHAPTER ONE

Outside Apprenticeship

"Well now," said Trevor, as he opened the door of his large corner flat off Sloane Square. "I was kind of expecting you."

"Must be the grape-vine," muttered Jon. "But don't question me too much, old man. I need more time to get myself together before I have a grilling."

Trevor peered at him closely and could see the defensive look in his friend's eye. The two men had known each other for many years, and each could equal the other in the number of pints downed in the evening and still remain sober enough to talk rationally. As a professional photographer Trevor was sensitive to expressions, so he watched Jon's face keenly. "Alright, alright. Come an' have some coffee. What about a beer? Where were you last night? Have you eaten?

"There you go," Jon chided. "Questions already, but I know you mean well. You've always been easy-going and undemanding. That's why I came to you. Quick answers first. Yes, I'd like some coffee. No beer at the moment, goes through the system too fast. I was here, there and everywhere last night and I don't need food. Does that give you all the answers?"

"Not giving much away, are you?" replied Trevor. "But your life's your own, and you must do what you must, but you would have known I'd have been upset when I heard that you'd left home. Knew something like that might happen. You've seemed uneasy for a long while. Wait a tick while I put the kettle on." He left the room to make the coffee, and while the kettle was boiling he cut some hefty cheese and pickle sandwiches. Jon looked around the large airy studio where electrical equipment was strewn about in a disorderly way. But there was nothing but orderliness and perfection in the work of the tall, dark quiet man.

When Trevor returned he found Jon sitting on the sofa fast asleep.

"Here you are, Jon. Here's the coffee." Jon woke up with a start.

"That's odd," he said. "I don't usually drop off like that. Must watch my step."

"Why have you come to see me?" asked Trevor, he made no mention of the sandwiches, but watched Jon tucking into them fast.

"It's like this," mumbled Jon with his mouth full. "Incidentally, touché over the grub. You win. Many thanks. I know you've heard by now that I've left all my past behind, and I think you know me well enough to understand the reason why. Don't chide me, Trev, don't make me have more guilty feelings than I make for myself. I must do what I have to do, and I must travel light in order to do this. What I am going to ask you is this. Could you look after this green rucksack for me and keep it very safe. I've had trouble enough carting the damn thing round looking for jobs. And when..."

"Wish you'd come sooner," interrupted Trevor. "I've been ever so worried, and..."

"It's got all my written work in it. All my poems..." Jon's voice faltered. "Suppose they'll be printed some day. But Trev, until I'm in a position to do anything properly I don't want anybody to read them. You can, if you like, just you. They're a bit scruffy, as I've jotted them down on any old bits of paper I could find. All the written work I have done is there, and over the years that has taken up a lot of my time and thoughts. Crumpled up, some of it, so parts of it you may not decipher. Will you do this for me?"

"Is that all you want? 'Course I will. Look, I'll put it in the top of that cupboard and keep it locked. Will that relieve your mind?"

"Thanks, that looks fine. My! That coffee was good. But, Trev, if you ever see anyone from Weybridge that knows me, tell them I'm safe and well, and please not to try and follow me." Jon paused, for he could not bring himself to mention his family. He looked at Trevor with puzzled eyes.

"O.K.," said Trevor. "I understand what you are saying and what you're not saying. I admire you, but I also think you are slightly peculiar going to such extreme lengths to prove your point."

"It's not just proving a point. I'm trying to change man's pattern of thinking and his values. I'm no angel, but a bit like yourself. I like my wine, my women, and my creature comforts." Both men laughed. "But the world scenario is getting too dangerous to let is slide further into chaos," Jon continued "and I must try to stop it. In whatever way I can. By whatever means. Understand me, Trev, and don't ask me anything more."

Jon made his way to the door. Trevor held out his hand in a spontaneous gesture of reassurance. "Whatever happens Jon, remember I'm here. Let me be your one link with your old life. You can use this flat as your home whenever you need or want to."

"I'll remember all you've said, and thanks for everything." Jon turned and ran down the stairway surprised to find he had tears in his eyes.

Must toughen myself, up. I'm such a softie inside. Ever since my orphanage days I've had to pretend to be tough. No tears allowed and that sort of thing. I was that soft when those louts robbed the nest of eggs and then catapulted the parent thrush. What a bloody nose they got from me! I don't like seeing people hurt and unhappy. Does me good to give them a leg up. Gave too much away, that's what

I did. But my family had everything they needed so I didn't mind. Suppose that could be one reason why I am here. Even my old faithful accountant couldn't rescue the mess I'd made of the financial side of Luminaire. My, I enjoyed designing. Getting the lighting effects just right. Wonderful feeling. But marketing the stuff wasn't my line. Too much bum-licking. Too much climbing over the next man. Too much deviousness.

He felt much freer without the heavier bag as he walked across the Park. His stomach was warm and full with the coffee and sandwiches, and the sun shone on his back. He found an empty bench and waited till it was time to go to Speaker's Corner, his mind still dwelling on his visit to Trevor. It was a Sunday morning in August. It was four days since he had cut adrift from the pressures of his previous life. In those four days he had looked around for part time work. After he had drawn blank in restaurants and hotels in the West End he went to pubs in the Knightsbridge area, selecting the ones that he had not been to in his previous life. He looked clean and tidy, and though middle-aged was strong and upstanding which hid the widening beer-drinking girth. Fortunately on the fourth day of job hunting he had been taken on at the Fox and Geese for the evening shift to clear the tables and wash up. Not too many questions were asked and he shrugged off those that were getting tiresome. He was to start at six and finish when the pub closed and his work was done, and he was allowed to help himself to food while working. He had carried the two bits of baggage everywhere, the heavier rucksack holding his work, and the smaller holdall with all his other possessions. His mind had plenty of time to wander. The sun played on his face as he sat and waited.

Now I've got to get myself in hand. I've got a job. That's fine, and I've got rid of the heavy rucksack. It make a good pillow those last few nights though. Good job it's August.

This three-quarter jacket wouldn't keep me warm in the winter. But it's got good pockets for my glasses. What else is in the pockets? Ah, yes. Pad and pencil, toilet paper, and some coppers. And my driving licence. Well, that'll be proof of my identity. It's the only proof I've got. And my bank book, right from the army days. Glory me, there's all of £300 in there. Will keep that for emergencies. Now where was I? It's good to have plenty of time to myself. No moping around though, missing the family. No regrets at winding up the business. I must, must, must satisfy this daemon that keeps driving me to find this change for a better world. I'll call it my social revolution. And I don't want any advantages like affluence, no privileges like security. No, no material assets either. I must find a way to individual integrity. Then I can speak about what I have found, write about what I have found. I want equality of dignity for the poor and rich, not for the poor and downtrodden to have to fight like I've had to fight. I want everyone to have a home, and feel safe in their homes and on the streets.

After mid-day he got up and walked slowly to Speaker's Corner. This Sunday there seemed a motley lot of speakers, the one who was attracting the most attention was a minister, clothed in black from head to foot, who was waving his arms, then pointing, then holding his hands heavenwards.

"Wonder what he's asking us to do or believe," Jon muttered to a stranger standing by him.

"God only knows," replied the stranger, a middle aged American who had cameras strung around his neck. "He seems to get worked up each time he comes, and I've been here often. Last Sunday he was blasting away at the flower power movement, the advent of drugs amongst the young people and the splitting up of families. So far it's one point I've agreed with him, the social upheaval of the sixties that we're all putting up with. Don't see eye to eye with much else he says. Too arrogant for me. His lot always seem to be begging. Personally, can't see what they've got to beg for, they're all well housed and well fed and goodness knows how much of the money they get is spent on those actually needing it. Mostly goes on pomp and ceremony and buildings, I think."

Jon was encouraged by these remarks. "I feel like asking some questions. First time I've done this," muttered Jon.

"Go on, have a go," urged his new acquaintance. "I'll wait and listen to you."

"Hi! Minister," called Jon. The minister looked Jon's way. "Yes, what's it you want? Are you ready to be called to God? Do you give thanks to Him for His great mercy?"

"Not so fast, sir, not so fast." Jon was prepared to be as polite as he could, taking off his cap and exposing his grey tinged red hair with large balding patch. "Firstly I want nothing. Secondly, I am not ready to be called to God, as you said. And thirdly I do not give thanks to Him for His great mercies in the way you expect me to." The crowd grew silent, and the Minister puffed under his breath.

"Well young man, it's about..."

Jon chipped in, laughing. "I'm not a young man, and well you can see it. I can probably give you a few years, but among other things what I want to know is why is it that under the protection of your black clothes do you and your colleagues continually ask those much poorer than yourselves for funds? Why do you make these good people feel guilty if they haven't contributed money that they can ill afford? I would call this a legal form of blackmail. Why can't you all give help and sustenance without expecting something in return?"

"That's putting it a bit steep, chum" said the American.

The minister paused for a moment, then turned away from Jon and said in a sonorous voice, "God's Will will be done. Now let us close by singing the hymn All Creatures that on Earth do Dwell'." He bellowed the first line, obviously proud of his singing ability. Jon moved away disgusted, muttering to the American.

"He never even answered my questions. S'pose I should take it a bit slower and get the crowd involved with question and answer if I'm to hold their interest."

"Best do that," replied the American. "I'll be here to listen if you come again."

"I might speak myself, you never know!" Jon replied with a smile, recovering his good humour.

"Sounds fine. See ya", and the American moved off into the crowd. Jon put his mind to thinking what his subject would be for debate while he strolled back across the Park in the warm afternoon sun. He was in no hurry for he had nowhere special to go. He bought tea in a plastic cup from a vendor and sat on the grass and watched the ducks. The grass was warm and smelt sweetly. There was a family playing football not far away.

Wonderful, wonderful grass. There you go, growing and growing. Nothing daunts you. Drought, gravel, floods. You pop up through them all. Even nature's enemy, concrete, doesn't defeat you. I wish the goodness of man was as resilient. Wish I could feel that soul could survive against all the modern distractions like the grass survives.

Watch it, lad! You nearly let in that goal. Good footwork that nipper's got. She's a typical mum, just busy with sorting out the picnic. Makes me a bit sad for they are just like my family. I must cover up the pain I feel when I remember my old life with the pain of uncertainty, with feelings of anticipation. Must live in the moment of 'now', and not look around for things that I haven't got. There is so much I used to want but didn't need. Now I must settle for things that I need... sleep, warmth, food. I must think positively, and help other people to do the same. People must feel good about themselves, that's another thing I must try to do, help people to feel good, not guilty or remorseful. God! What a world.

He laughed aloud enjoying some memories, and the nearby

footballer gave him a quizzical look.

I must be an odd bastard, laughing to myself. That young lad gave me such a funny look.

The footballer, all of twelve years, called out, "Hi, mister, come and 'ave a kick." Jon was delighted, and for the next hour kicked the ball around with the family. "You sure know some tricks," said the twelve year old. "Where did you learn 'em?"

"A long time ago," replied Jon. "When the ball was made of leather, and it was very heavy when it rained. Fair knocked your head about if you didn't time it right. Hard boots we wore too, nothing like the light things you've all got now. Up against a wall, I learnt my tricks, kicking at an exact spot up against a wall." Jon's memory flashed back to the days in the Orphanage when he spent hours on his own with the ball making it do just what he wanted to do. The father in the family started to help his wife pack up.

"Must go now," he said. "Perhaps we'll see you next week. We're usually here."

"Perhaps," replied Jon, but even in his mind he would make no commitment. He didn't want to be tied to a social engagement however trivial. He put the feeling of envy he had for the small family well to the back of his mind.

That night he worked a good shift, chatting freely to the customers as he cleared the tables. There was no time to sit down for his food, so he ate as much as he could while standing doing the washing up. Nobody minded, nobody took much notice of him as long as he kept up with the chores that were expected of him. He drew himself a pint, which he paid for, and had another after closing time which the landlord stood him.

"Been watching you," said the landlord. "You seem to have the gift of the gab, talking to everyone. Let them have the last word sometimes, makes them feel good. But

I like your style. Been around a bit have you? Been doing better things, eh?"

"I'm not here to be quizzed, and I don't like it," Jon muttered crossly. "I'm here to give good service. Too much prying and I'm off."

"Sorry, chum, sorry. Hint taken. We'll let things be, shall we?" The landlord looked a bit puzzled. "See you tomorrow," he called after Jon who was putting on his jacket.

"O.K.," said Jon. "Goodnight all, see you tomorrow," and he stepped out into the night.

Where to now? My blasted bladder. Must learn to control it. Public conveniences are so far apart, but I must use trees and lamp posts as little as possible. But what else is there to do when I'm taken short?

He puzzled about this as he walked towards Paddington station in the hope of getting a cup of tea from the station restaurant.

Must find the places that are going to be open through the night. It's alright now, but I'll need something hot in the winter months. In spite of the beer I'm needing another cuppa. Will have a try at Paddington. Cor, my legs aren't half aching.

He rested on a low wall, half of his journey to the station completed. This was the outer wall of a superior block of flats, which were well lit. The car park was full.

Wonder what's going on in there, who is loving who, and who is pretending to love? Are they having a blazing row over something they feel strongly about? If so, can they apologize or do they have to bluff and pretend that all the time they are right? Are they big enough to say sorry to each other if they have hurt? Do they give each other space to be individuals and do they live able to compromise? Why am I thinking that there should be two people, man and wife? Lonely people, old and sad, could be behind those curtains, or two men as partners, or two women. Is any one there to help them? Or does their money provide all that is necessary? What do they all think of? Are they fearful of tomorrow dwelling in the past as an escape? Or are they planning the next move up the materialistic ladder?

I've never had time to think like this before, I've been too busy with my work and my poetry. Do thought waves help this need for change? I dunno yet. Wonder if I could help people to base their values on truth if their priorities would change. My favourite word, 'lifemanship', would flourish. Lust wins the battle now.

Jon was far away in the recesses of his own mind when he was rudely brought back to the present moment, "Evening Sir. Must ask you to move on. Been 'ere some while, 'aven't yer. What yer lookin' at?"

Jon's hackles rose. What harm was he doing sitting on a wall? "Evening, constable." Jon purposely did not refer to the three stripes on the policeman's arm. "I'm looking at a brick wall with windows in it. What do yer think about that?" Jon naughtily copied the policeman's accent.

"Don't give me lip," said the policeman tetchily. "Move on now, move along, please."

"Course I'll move on. But I'd think you'd have better things to do than bother someone who is minding their own business. Who pays you to look for thieves and robbers who are not minding their own business but poking their noses into other people's property? I suppose it's easier for you to harass people like myself, than picking a fight with a tough 'un."

As Jon walked off he saw the policeman write something in his pad. It was past midnight when he arrived at Paddington Station. The main restaurant was closed, so he bought some hot chocolate from the vending machine. His feet throbbed and his back ached and he needed sleep, so he walked the length of a side platform and found an empty trailer that was used for carrying the post. He pushed it in the lee of a small hut so that he could not be seen from the main booking office, and sat in a hunched position, head on knees. He woke shortly, rigid from sitting in a curved position, his hands and feet tingling with pins and needles. His bladder was at bursting point. He relieved himself against the hut.

Damn that beer and chocolate. Can't last till morning, and I don't want to be seen back at the gents. If it's this cold in August, what's it going to be like in the winter months? I've already had my first brush with the law, and blow me, I wasn't doing anything wrong. 'Spose I'd better watch my step. Better try for some more sleep.

He climbed back on the trolley, and in spite of the cold dropped off to sleep again. The sun was shining on his face when he woke next with the first train clattering into the adjacent platform. He climbed stiffly off the trolley, and walked down the length of the platform, keeping out of sight as much as possible.

"Had a good sleep?" Jon was surprised to hear a voice calling. It was the train driver. "Woke you up, didn't I?" the driver called out laughingly. "Best hop it quick, the watchers start arriving about now."

"Thanks mate, I'm just off", Jon replied. The driver was an elderly man with a round lined face. "Got any tips for a good place for a night's kip? Don't want to cause any trouble", Jon continued.

"Not really, sir", replied the driver. "But some on the gate are softer than others. Just have to chat 'em up maybe. Take care of yourself". The driver turned away to fiddle with some knobs.

Why did he call me sir? I suppose I still look quite respectable and don't appear to be homeless. Won't last for long. God,

I'm longing for some tea and a smoke. Those are the last things I'm going to do without, tea, smoking and my beer.

With these thoughts Jon carefully approached the restaurant, making it appear he had come in from a side entrance. Luckily he found he was not the first customer, and he settled down to tea and a cigarette. It was not long before he was in conversation with early travellers, and he seemed allowed to stay as long as he liked. But he was soon to find he was not going to have such a smooth passage at the Fox and Geese.

Chapter Two

Working and Speaking

Jon had been at the Fox and Geese for three weeks. He found the work adequate, but tension rose each night. The barmaid, a sultry woman, skinny and flat both back and front, make it clear that she wanted to date her fellow worker.

"Cum arn, toots, don't say you can't cum wiv me tonight. Not again. You said that last night." She grinned close to his face as he passed the bar counter balancing a load of dirty plates on his arm. Jon was getting angry with her. Part of him shirked from hurting her feelings, part of him rejected her thin form, and the smell of beer and stale clothes.

"Yer funkie, yer are. Oi won't 'urt yer. Got a nice place, Oi 'ave. Why don't yer come fer a drink?" She went on goading him.

"I'm busy," Jon replied. "Even when I've finished here I've got work to do."

"Work, my foot. Bet all yer do is bend yer elbow. Bet yer got a cunt waiting fer yer. Pretendin' to be all goody-goody. Alrigh'. Won't ask yer again. Shammer, that's wot yer look loike." She banged a glass of beer on the counter, and it spilled. Customers were looking her way, laughing, enjoying the spectacle. "Just a bloody shammer." Jon said nothing, took his coat off the hook, and went to find the boss.

"My money, please. As much as you owe me, and no more. I'm not going to put up with this abuse."

"Sorry, Jon," spluttered the landlord. "I've been watching what's been going on. That woman's a fool, but she's a good worker and the locals like her. I'll miss you. Got used to your funny ways. You seemed to attract the customers." He said no more for he saw the rage in Jon's face. Jon left by the back door, still angry.

Shammer. Me, a shammer! That's the last thing I am. Blast that bloody woman. Right upset me, it has. My whole life I've worked against that sort of thing.

He walked down two more streets, and went into another pub where he sat in a corner, and drank himself into a stupor. He was led out at closing time, and then zigzagged down the road. He found a small alleyway, and spotted a dustbin and a wooden crate. He sat jerkily on the crate, leaning on the dustbin, too full of drink to appreciate his situation. Several hours later an inquisitive cat looking for food disturbed him.

Lucky it isn't the law. Come on puss, let me give you a tickle. I really am trespassing this time, but I haven't hurt anything, but I feel all wet. Oh hell, I've peed myself. Still, can't be helped. It'll soon dry off the ground and won't show. Must find a bath and a hot drink to clear my head. Is this what life is going to be like? For ever and ever like this? Lucky I've got money, money enough for a bath and a tip to the attendant to let me wash my clothes. Won't take long if I can use the hot pipes to dry things on.

He walked slowly towards Victoria, and the public baths, his mouth feeling like a bird cage with his head throbbing. After a long soak in soothing hot water and a general clean up, the longed for cup of tea tasted like nectar. Apart from the episode at the Fox and Geese the first month had gone smoothly. He had no other confrontations, and had time to watch the crowds at Speaker's Corner and think of a core for his first long speech. He knew it was time for him to speak and he knew he must find another job.

It was the second Sunday in September at midday when he stood on a small box, a little way from the other people, who were listening to the other tub thumpers. He said nothing for some moments, just chatted quietly to a few of the crowd who had gathered.

Then he spoke. "Good morning my friends, and hello. Today I want to talk about 'Revolutionaries." He paused for a moment watching the interest deepening in the faces before him.

"That's a rum start," called a voice from the back of the crowd.

"Never mind that, but 'Revolutionaries' is a word that sometimes makes people afraid. Communism, Fascism, Neo-Nazism, all these names come to the fore. I'm for none of that. I'm for change, change that leads to truth." Another short pause.

"Goin' to be a gas-bag, are yer?", chipped in the same voice.

Jon disregarded the interruption. "The old revolutionaries who hit the headlines with what they called truth are labelled wrongly. Their aims were wrong, their values were wrong, and their priorities were wrong. But they have one thing in common, they have lied and they still lie, but they lie differently."

Jon paused. He heard murmurs in the crowd which was swelling at the edges. Stern poker faced men were watching.

Wonder who they are? Plain clothes police? Informers? They look like the Gestapo, same shape, different clothes, same stern faces. Wonder if they'd give me the same treatment that I had in the cells? Rifle butting, cigarette burning, the lot. Damn it, I was only a boy. Don't expect I could put up with that hard regime at my age.

Before he could continue with his speech he had to put those thoughts out of his mind.

"Cum arn, tell us 'ow different. Lie is a lie. Can't fiddle

'bart wi' tha'".

Again Jon continued ignoring the interruption. "The true and the real revolutionary works in a different way. They are the old and young and in-betweens. Nurses, who work long hours for love rather than money, doctors who slave through the night without any recognition, people who care steadfastly and selflessly for the old and infirm without support or financial help. I'm sure most of you have come across these silent heros." He looked across the sea of faces and saw some nodding sagely.

"That's like me Elsie here." A stout onlooker put his arm round his even stouter wife.

"That's fine," replied Jon, nodding to the stout man. Then he continued, "but I've never known a bookmaker who was a revolutionary." There was a small laugh from the crowd. Jon explained, "The revolutionary who I classify as useful to humanity at large does not need a five minute yelling spree in front of the media, kicking in a copper's head, breaking windows or burning homes. Those bastards reach the bastard class long before verbal violence is committed. These morons have been aggravated into this brutal form of expression either because they can't make out fully in life as an individual or because they are deranged."

"'Oo yer pointin' finger at, Mister?"

Jon disregarded the same nagging voice from the back of the crowd. "My form of revolutionary is for the young to show respect for the old, to go through the door last, and get up in a bus if there's no spare seat. It is for the old to encourage and enjoy the efforts of the young, not to mock their ideas and laugh at their different habits, their informal clothes. This is a small and easy way for change. There are many others." He paused again.

The stout man and his Elsie both murmured, "Hear, hear."

"But I think you must all agree that the only reason for change is that there must be a better quality of life for all." He looked around, there were nods of assent. "Now, we seem to agree that change is needed. I must add strongly that change is needed now and that change must be drastic. There must be a universal time limit. I would suggest a year. In this year there must be a cessation of all violent activities on a global scale. The needs of people are real and an immediate start on those needs must be begun. Trade and commerce could be re-assessed giving priority to those at the bottom of the pile, and by peeling off needless costs put on by managements and those in control." Jon paused, waiting for comments. "Voluntary hostages could be held in complex areas to ensure the safety of national ethnic and religious interests. Wars on behalf of God should be abandoned. We should speak with a World authority."

The crowd were very quiet, save for the voice from the back. "Load 'o balls. Load 'o balls. Wish Oi'd stayed 'ome."

"Sssh, sssh," hissed a section of the crowd near him.

Jon finished his speech in a low voice. He said slowly, "Justice is only done when it is really done for rich and poor alike. Slip off your role of manipulator of mankind, and become the servant of mankind. Then you will know the personal cost of a true revolution. I say to you, **start now**. It is the only way to stop the slide into chaos." He stepped down off his box, and slipped away, tired with his efforts. He realised that he had still given the crowd little opportunity to enter a discussion, that he had talked at them, not involved them.

Maybe I'll get better. I've never spoken to an unknown crowd before. Only addressed a crowd of military when I was in Intelligence. That was different. Only factual. Must go carefully now, till I'm sure of a job and more money. Don't really fancy sleeping in the open tonight. Although its only September it's quite chilly. Could be real cold before dawn. Think I'll try the trains at Victoria. Try for a kip in one that is being cleaned. If I lie low they may not spot me.

He walked along the curved road down to the station, Buckingham Palace tucked securely behind the high spiked walls on one side, hotels and clubs in tall well built houses on the other. An elderly man, hat lop-sided and collar of his coat tucked in, joined him. "Wouldn't be in the Queen's place for a million pounds," Jon said, feeling the temperature of the stranger's monarchistic feelings.

"She's alright," the man muttered, a cigarette hanging sloppily from his lip. "It's the hangers on. Too much money spent on 'em. Could do with a corner in one of their palaces. Queen Mum's my favourite. Bless 'er 'eart."

"Overall, I think they earn their living," Jon countered. "Think how much money they attract by tourism. There's no other country with so much pomp and ceremony. We put on a show better than anywhere, and it's only because we've a Monarch. Lots of people envy us. And think of all the stress they have, and all that ghastly formality."

"S'pose you're right. Proper monarchist aren't you? Well, what do you think of the swell people that lives in them houses?" The stranger pointed to the large houses with well lit high ceilinged rooms. "Only half a mile away you've got the poor and the likes of me in bed and breakfast. Reckon things should be more equal. It's a long time since I had a Sunday dinner. 'Cor, I couldn't half do with some roast beef and Yorkshire pudding, and gravy, lots and lots of gravy." The cigarette fell to the ground, and the man left it on the pavement.

Filthy habit. I'll promise to myself never to leave anything around, not even a matchstick. Can't make you out, old boy. You don't talk too badly, and your trousers are ironed, but you are so untidy. You're younger than me. Been turned out of home? Can't tell. Why the bed and breakfast? Feel you've got a lot of angry feelings tucked away inside you. Don't want to be saddled with him all evening. I'll offer him a cuppa, and say I've only half an hour free.... Hell, no.... That wouldn't be the truth. I've the whole effing evening with nothing to do. Wonder if he knows I'm dossing. Don't think so. Still feel a bit tetchy about it, sort of ashamed.

"I'm off to the station. Come and have a cuppa while I wait?"

"Thanks ever so, but no. Must get to my lodgings and claim the bed I like the best. I always go for the one by the window. With five in the room the beds at the back get stuffy." Jon's temporary companion shuffled off passed St. Michael's Church. Jon spent a long time in the station restaurant, writing on his pad and watching the crowd. He talked to anyone who sat by him, they all seemed self-sufficient and interested only in their own worlds. It was a long Sunday evening without the hustle and bustle of the rush hour. He saw a group of porters standing round a dark old fashioned brazier at the side of the platform. He walked up to them slowly.

"Evening," he called, testing the wavelengths.

"Evening, sir," replied a cheerful grubby man.

"Don't call me sir," Jon laughed. "In the state that I am I don't even qualify to be called mister."

It was the turn of the three men to laugh. "Want a warm up? What about a cuppa? No hurry, are you?"

Jon instantly felt these men could be his allies. A large enamel mug brimming with strong sweet tea was put into his hands. In return Jon passed his packet of cigarettes around. Conversation flowed evenly, sometimes there was silence but it was not uneasy. Talk was about their homes, their duty hours, and their beer. No politics, no acrimony. They seemed content with their lot. Waves of relief swept over him, for these good people took him as he was, no questions, no probing. After a long while Jon left them. The station was emptying, and this time he did not feel like incriminating the men should he be found on railway premises at an unauthorised time. He moved on towards the embankment. The cold air made him realise that he had not eaten properly all day, and that his half jacket was not a match for the night air.

He had another smoke and curled up on a bench. Shortly another figure appeared, well muffled. He could not see if it was male or female. He could only smell a smell of a dirty human being. It took him back to the days to his prison camp in Poland when water was short and the weather hot, and there were too many men crammed together, smelling of unwashed bodies. The muffled figure sat on the next bench and stretched its legs. From the size of the broken down boots Jon knew it was a man.

"Like a smoke, chum?" Jon called.

"Like 'ell oi would," answered the form on the bench. "Jest finished me last." Jon crossed over and helped the man to light up. All that was visible in the night light was a pair of bloodshot eyes peeping out of a fringe of hair. They were not old eyes, just eyes full of puzzlement. Jon returned to his bench where he could get the weight of his body off his legs. He was close enough to hold a conversation. He talked to the young man, but soon realised that it was the young man who wanted to talk to him. For several hours the youngster talked, sadly, bitterly, and sometimes poetically. From his command of the spoken word, Jon assessed he had been well educated. Jon interjected a few words, but he felt it was the listening that mattered. Strangely the young man broke off in the middle of a sentence, and Jon realised that he had fallen asleep. Jon tried to do the same but with not much success. He smoked and shivered, got up and stamped his feet, and sat down again in a different position. Sleep eluded him.

*My! It's taking a long time for dawn. This **is** a lesson to me. It's only autumn. What's it going to be like midwinter? Must try to doss down on a full stomach. And work, blooming work. That's top priority.*

Leaving the youngster, with only his forehead showing, still asleep, Jon peed in some nearby rhododendron bushes and then walked to Picadilly and found a Lyon's restaurant opening up. There were several people who appeared as unshaven as he was, so he did not feel out of place. He ordered tea and a bacon sandwich and took as long as he could to eat it. It was only when the young lad came fluttering at his table with a dirty white cloth to clear the crockery that he got up to go to the toilets, where he emptied his bowels.

That's a good job done. That's going to be a bit of a problem now. Peeing is easy, but this needs some negotiating. There's nobody here, so I am going to have a jolly good wash and shave. Lucky I don't have to shave every day with my beard. Ah! What's this for an idea. I'm sure I could do just as well as that young lad with the dirty cloth. I could clear tables. Did it in the pub. I'll try here and see if there's a vacancy. Big enough concern. Must have a large turnover. Nothing to be lost in trying.

Still carrying his small holdall he went into the main hall and asked at the glass fronted desk. "Well, sir, what can I do for you?" There stood a young girl, smartly dressed, with large sad eyes.

"I was looking for the Personnel Manager. I'm wondering if you have a vacancy for a waiter for any part of the day. I've previous experience." Jon did not say that his previous experience was nearly forty years ago when he worked as a lad in a Leeds hotel.

"I'm the Personnel Manager for those looking for temporary employment. Come into my office and sit down."

"I was expecting somebody longer in the tooth than you," laughed Jon as he sat on the leather chair. "Mind if I smoke?"

"Well, truthfully I don't like it, but if you must, you can. There's no smoking in the restaurant area and in the kitchens. Does that make any difference to wanting a job?" The young girl looked at Jon keenly, obviously trying to work out how and why he was sitting in front of her asking for a menial job.

"No, I want work." Jon paused. "I want work where I can be left alone to get on with it. What have you got to offer?"

This girl studied her chart. "Well," she said after a pause, "I've got a vacancy from 7am till 2pm, six days a week, or from 6pm till midnight. That's six days a week too. Both sessions there's half an hours break when you can get a free meal in the staff canteen. They're both for clearing and washing up. We don't put people straight on to serving 'til we see how they work out. Are you sure this is what you want?" The girl looked quizzically at Jon. "It's flat rates only, doesn't come to much but it would be regular money."

"I'll take the morning shift," Jon replied straight away. "Suit me fine. But what do I call you? Don't feel like calling you Madam, and can't call you Miss as you've got a ring on your finger?"

"Most of the temps call me Mrs Baines, 'cept the older ones. They call me Kate. I think you come into that category, don't you?" and she gave a whimsical smile. Jon saw sadness flash across her face as she handed the papers across the table to sign.

"Just a formality. I'm here myself till two-thirty, then I have to go home. Let me know if you want anything. You can start tomorrow on level four. I'll warn the kitchen superintendent."

"You'll get good service from me as long as I'm left alone and not bossed about too much. I'm just an ordinary guy who can't go through any door without it being open, and I can't work miracles."

Kate laughed. "You'll do. I'm sure you'll do. Excuse me now, I've got to go to a meeting. Maybe I'll see you tomorrow. You'll be given an overall."

Jon walked slowly down the wide shallow concrete stairs, and stepped out onto the pavement.

Now let's see how I stand. Morning work, that's good. One meal, that's better. Must get tidy before I arrive, that's not so good. Good toilet facilities, that's good. No smoking, that's difficult. And I wonder why that Kate has such a sad look. I feel quite lighthearted, no more competition, no more having to live surrounded by pretence. It's up to me, and me alone, how I work for this revolutionary change. Must look out for the needs of anyone I come across. Must keep myself open to eye signals.

The work kept Jon on the move, but he was quite relaxed. Between 11am and 11.30am he went for his break, and had a good meal. Often he saw Kate sitting alone, staring out of the window. She seemed quite detached.

After Jon had worked for two weeks he saw Kate, alone again, and again staring out of the window with her large serious eyes.

"Do you mind if I sit here with you?" Jon asked. "I think my age gives me the liberty to break conventions, don't you?"

"Yes, yes, do come." Kate was pleased to see him. "I've had good reports about you. You've made a great hit with the rest of the staff."

"It's not that I want to talk about. It's that you look so sad. I've watched you looking out of the window, just looking so sad. Is there anyway I could be of help?"

Kate's eyes misted over. "No one has ever noticed that before. Yes, Jon, I AM sad. That's the reason why I have to go home for the afternoon. I feel I can't leave Jack, he's my husband, for too long." Kate paused, and Jon felt she needed some encouragement before she could continue.

"Things not alright there?" Jon asked so opening up the dialogue.

"We're fine between us. There's nothing wrong between us. You mustn't think there is. I love that man, and always will. But last month he lost his job, got the accounts into a muddle. His boss is saying it's all his fault. Jack is a dreamer, he's not suited for accounting and tidy factual work. Don't know why his parents made him take up that line. And now he can't get a job and he feels a failure. He hates being dependent on me, and is getting more and more morose. He hates being on his own. It just seems to go round and round. Oh dear, why am I talking to you like this?"

"Because I asked you to, my dear. I felt there was something that was troubling you. I am where I am because I didn't fit, so I can understand a bit how he feels. Perhaps he isn't a failure at all, perhaps he is learning to live if he can see things in perspective."

"He's such a worrier, worrying what his parents will think, and what the neighbours will say when they go on seeing him at home all day and me going out to work," Kate's forehead crinkled into small lines, all the semblance of efficiency as a Personnel Manager slipping away.

"That's where you come in, Kate," replied Jon. "Love him as he is and for what he is. Give him back his self-esteem. It doesn't matter if he doesn't go back to accountancy if he is more at peace with the world doing something else. Why should he be made to work at something that leads to failure? For those learning to live I give a toast. Pity it's only in tea!" There was a pause. Jon looked at his watch. "That crowd in there'll think I'm sucking up to the boss, better I go and finish the piles of dirty dishes." Kate was still sitting silently, but now a small smile played around her lips. "Goodbye," she said quietly, "and thanks."

Jon went back to the sink, the place was very quiet and the superintendent looked at him angrily. Cheekily Jon looked at his watch, "I've been away thirty one and a half minutes. Going to make a fuss of that?"

"It's not usual for the kitchen staff to sit with the Personnel Manager. Stay with your own kind."

"Don't you tell me how to behave," Jon snapped. "Tell me what to do as far as the job goes. That's all. I'm not a sheep playing follow-my-leader. There's not one person here that's been hurt by me. How many people feel uncomfortable and unimportant after you've been speaking to them?" There were a few sniggers from the tables. The superintendent was not a popular man. Jon felt he had said enough for one day. "Now just let me get on with my work, and you get on with yours." Jon went through the swing doors, picked up a tray and went to the main restaurant.

"You pricked that fellow's bubble," mumbled one of the fellow staff as they passed in the narrow space between the tables.

"Shouldn't take advantage of his position," Jon whispered. "We're all just people inside. Why not talk to anyone and everyone. Must off. Young beady eyes is watching." Jon moved on collecting more and more dirty plates, smiling and quipping with the customers.

Must watch myself with that conceited pompous ass. Wonder how long I can stick his pettiness. Pity, the job suits me fine, but I'm not going to kow-tow to the likes of him. Time for off. Good-oh. Wonder what will happen in these next few days?

CHAPTER THREE

Unscheduled Journey

It was Sunday morning in mid-December. Jon was still working at Lyons, but the tension was rising between him and the superintendent. He sat in the cold sun in St James's Park watching the ducks; they looked tattered and forlorn. Although he was hungry he felt at peace with the world. The leather coat with detachable lining that he had bought from Oxfam kept him warm.

Decent old girl, that one who sold me my coat. Brought the price down too. Spare trousers as well, good and warm they are, and the gloves and scarf. All for an extra pound. Means more for me to carry round. Never mind, I can always wear them all! What a sight I would look! Can't go on long with that damned superintendent. I see in him all that I despise. Now what am I going to speak about this afternoon?... Must have a think.... The last few Sundays have been easy just getting the crowd interested in everyday events. Want to get them used to seeing me. Several of them seem to wait for me to come. Angry people too, some of them. Wonder what's made them like that?

The crowds were small that Sunday at Speaker's Corner, so Jon waited hoping that more would arrive during the afternoon.

Soon he stood on his box and began to speak. "I've been talking to these good people just now," he said pointing to part of the crowd, "and there seems a sense of anxiety, a lack of purpose. Most of you lead a comfortable life with adequate money and many too many possessions."

"Don't you be telling me wot I should 'ave and wot I shouldn't. None of your business," shouted an angry voice.

Jon took no notice. He continued, "how many of you have bought something you don't really need because your neighbour has it? How many have traded in a perfectly good car and bought a bigger and more powerful one, and so giving yourselves a feeling of one-up-manship?"

"Worse than a bleedin' sermon," the same voice interrupted.

Regardless, Jon continued. "I've done it myself, it's part of human nature to be greedy. Don't we all use as much water as we want without thinking where it comes from? Don't we all use paper and all that is made from wood without a thought of the trees, trees that could be performing their natural function if they weren't felled to supply millions of books, papers and magazines for millions of people? I'm sure you've been harangued about this through television, through the newspapers, and from charities."

There were nods from the crowd. "You bet we have," came a voice from the far edges. "What you on about?"

"This is what I'm on about," retorted Jon. "I'm not going on talking about things that the medias do. That's for those who make money out of telling you. I am going to talk about just you and me, individuals sometimes seemingly of no importance, but who are really the most important thing of all."

There was a pause, and into the silence a quieter voice murmured, "Come on, tell us. Why are we so important?"

Jon pronounced his words slowly, "There are no actions inside yourselves superior to harmony, for all the energy converted in unity spells liberation. Don't be afraid to broaden the meaning of relationship even if it means flowing against current ideas. Refuse the options that in hurt and misery add to the obscenity of living." Jon watched carefully to see if the change of style in his language was being well received. The crowd looked interested. "In resolving discord, increase your awareness, so that with unity the value of all experience will be heightened, and those fortunate enough to come within your path will reflect a hope and gladness, and those unfortunate enough to have limits placed by themselves on life, will through your presence realise their limits were less than the truth."

The crowd remained silent, save for one elderly man who muttered loudly, "Not heard stuff like this before. Seems he's got a bit of sense."

"Can't understand 'arf. Nuthin but words. Streams of words", a high pitched voice whined.

Again Jon took no notice of the interruptions. "May you all live in harmony for the rest of your lives, and be able to know what it means to love and be loved in this hungry world. May you stay resurgent as the vital grass which blooms regardless of the devious demands upon it. Just BE." He paused again. "And where ever you are be at home, be at home even just within yourselves."

"Bit pompous ain't 'e?"

"I dunno. Maybe 'es got a point."

Murmuring the crowd gradually moved away, more quietly than usual as if contemplating the words they had just heard, words very different from the political or religious exhortations that they usually received. Jon was hungry for he had not eaten any food all day. He had existed on tea and cigarettes.

Going to have a jolly good blow-out. Feel a bit of a devil. Haven't touched that money yet in the bank, my paltry earnings off the Boxing Booth. Fancy a lad of fifteen saving money and keeping it till my age! Little it may be, but it's all I've got. Left the rest behind - glad I did though. Won't use it all - keep it for emergencies. Still got a bit in my pocket. Must cut down on the beer, that costs too much. but where am I to go and sit these dark evenings? Pubs are the only place for the likes of me with no roof of my own. They are a kind of sitting room for me, and I enjoy meeting a lot of different people. Perhaps they'll remember some of the things I say. Must stand a round or two, can't always be on the receiving end. Like hell, I'm hungry. Could eat a cart horse. Takes me back to my days in the prison camps. 250 calories a day for three months. That got a bit of getting used to. But I managed it. I'll manage this lot too. I'm not being beaten by the guards like I was then. Damned if I'm going to be brow beaten by that runt of a supervisor. Going to chuck it in tomorrow.

With this decision to leave the job at Lyons firmly made, Jon entered the Black Boy in Victoria Street. He sat by himself at a table by the window where he could watch the door, and ordered a bottle of stout and a plate of sausages, chips and cabbage.

Always like to see who's coming in and going out. Must have an escape route for myself. God, how good it smells when you're hungry. I'm watering at the mouth like a blooming dog! At least I can't look too scruffy and can't be smelling or these dames wouldn't have joined me.

Two middle aged women in head scarves came and sat at his table, Jon moved up to make more space. The two women talked across the table to each other, mouths full or empty they went on talking. They took no notice of Jon, who ate his meal in silence, cleaning the plate with an extra piece of bread. He ordered a second bottle of stout, and lent back. As the two women were smoking he did the same without asking. He was alone, but not lonely. Again he was at peace with himself.

He left at closing time, and went in the side entrance of Victoria Station. It was very empty, and Jon felt he might be conspicuous if he looked purposeless. He went straight to the gents toilet, peed, and had a hurried wash. He liked to clean his teeth as often as he could. As he came out of the toilets he saw one of the three men, one of his friends who had given him tea several weeks ago.

"Hello, sir," The station worker called. "Remember me?

What 'ave you bin up to?"

"I've been going here and there." There was a pause. Then Jon decided to try his luck. "Any ideas?"

The worker knew what Jon was implying. "The furthest one over there," and he gave a tiny nod with his head and moved off. "See you again," he said softly.

"Thanks chum," said Jon under his breath. The worker could see what Jon needed and wanted, he was an ally. Jon wanted a sleep for the night on a train where he wouldn't be disturbed. Great care had to be taken crossing the large station area, the station police had a habit of popping around at unscheduled times. Jon kept in the shadows moving slowly a bit at a time. He reached the train and moved cautiously along it. There was no one about. He came to the first class carriages, which were near the front of the train next to the mail van. They were beautifully warm, and he lay full length on the wide seat, taking care to keep his feet off the fabric. He rolled a cigarette, bending low to light it to make sure the flame of the match did not show out of the window.

I'm trespassing, that's what I'm doing. Hell, what does it matter? I'm not hurting anyone, I'm not going to vandalise anything. I just want to keep warm, and get off my feet. Like a blinking first class hotel this is. All I need now is a pillow, and some music and it would be like the Ritz. It's a long time ago since I spent a night there. My! What a turn around. Must watch these feet of mine. Swelling up too much. Never had that before 'cept in that darned camp. Couldn't get me boots on then, all swollen up I was. Gave me clogs instead, they did. Must have looked a sight, but they were warm enough when I wrapped my feet in paper. S'pose I'm standing up too long every day. Wonder why all these memories are coming back to me? Those memories of being a prisoner. Haven't thought about it for ages. Damn, I'm not alone.

At that moment of his ruminations, Jon saw a shadow slip past the corridor window. He hid his cigarette in the cup of his hand. Then the door opened.

"Ullo, Guv. Been watching yer for some time. Can I cum in? I'm on the same side as yer, yer know. Followed yer up across station, all along train, and yer never saw me."

Into the carriage came a tiny man, with the brightest black eyes Jon had ever seen. He seemed like a busy restless bird, with a beaklike nose that poked into everything. He pulled out a half bottle of whiskey, took a swig and handed the remains over to Jon.

"Thanks, mate," said Jon, choking slightly over a large gulp. "Come and sit down. Why have you been watching me?" He handed back the bottle.

"Seen yer in the Park, talkin' to all those people. Seen yer on the Underground, Circle line going round and round, seen yer in the other Park watching them ducks. Got a lot o' time on yer 'ands, 'aven't yer? What's it all 'bout, Guv, trying to change the world? Never nicked from you, Oi 'aven't. Thought yer be one of us." The little man talked in a steady stream, so Jon butted in.

"I mind my own business, that's what I do." The little man laughed. "But I don't like things as they are. I don't like the way the rich feed off the poor, I don't like the way the Government members line their own pockets while dishing out paltry sums for those in need. I don't like people having to live in fear of bombs, and I don't like it when ordinary people, that doesn't include a whippersnapper like you," again the little man chuckled, Jon repeated himself, "when ordinary people can't walk the streets safely, and I don't like the effect all this drug taking is having. Those are some of the things I don't like, and that I'm trying to change. And as I'm not going round throwing bombs or shooting people all I can do is talk and persuade. That's what I'm doing, and I'm trying to do it round the clock whenever the opportunity arises, and mark you, the occasions arise at most peculiar times and in peculiar places. Now, is that enough? And what is it that you say you do? I don't for one minute expect you to tell me the truth, but never mind. You seem to have enough time on your hands, and you appear to have money in your pocket. That coat of yours must have cost a mint."

"Well, Guv, Oi'd be in the nick for a ninety-nine year stretch if Oi'd bin caught for all the things Oi've took. Good trade it is. But yer safe, Guv. Yer safe. Won't take from yer. Yer be one of us now, Guv. Loike yer style. Coming to 'ear yer speak next Sunday. Wish there were more like yer. Them folks that listen to yer seem to want more. Can't make yer out meself. Where's money in it? My last copper went on Magic Jon on the two thirty at Newbury. Fell two from the front, and he were leading. Bet jockey was told not to let him win. Now Oi'm skint."

Jon stretched himself out again, hoping the little man would take a hint that it was sleep he wanted, not talk. The little man did just that and slipped out of the carriage closing the door, his soft shoes made no noise at all. "See yer Guv. See yer tomorra."

Me, one of them? Do I really look like that? A thief? Why, I've never stolen from anyone. Hope I don't see him tomorrow. But in a way, I like his cheekiness.

Jon closed his eyes and sleep rolled over him like an anaesthetic aided by the stout and the warm carriage. He slept so deeply that he did not feel the train starting to move. He only woke when it was light, a soft light of early dawn. He sat up with a start, and looked out of the window.

That's Guilford Cathedral, I'm damn sure that's Guilford Cathedral. We're probably heading for Portsmoutb. And I haven't got a ticket, and I'm jolly well not going to pay for a return journey that I don't even want. Got to use my wits now. Must pee first, that's top priority.

He opened the door, and saw no one. He walked along the corridor, head up, carrying his bag as if he was a legitimate passenger. He passed by the mail van and looked in. There he saw the little man, the thief, his visitor of last night, rummaging amongst the mail bags. There was a half opened parcel on the floor.

Jon called out, "What **are** you up to?"

"Don't yer loike it, Guv?"

"I bloody well do not." Jon answered tersely. "You could get both our collars felt if you're caught." He turned away, but as he did so he saw the thief open the window and toss out the half opened parcel. Early though it was Jon managed to perform both his functions in the first class toilet, and he had a scrape of a shave. It took about ten minutes. Then he walked back along the corridor. In the first of the compartments he saw the thief.

"Come in, Guv, come in. We've got to look slippy to get out o' this lot. Reckon we 'op out at 'avant, track side, and 'ope no one is looking. No good getting all the way to Portsmouth. If yer act proper we might be taken for track workers."

"Not in that coat, you won't," interjected Jon. "Well, hung for a sheep as for a lamb, we're breaking the law already, might as well do as you say." He had a sneaking liking for the thief's audacity, and he was starting to enjoy flaunting the fringes of authority.

"Make sure yer shut the door behind yer," advised the thief.

"Know your way about, don't you? Done this before, haven't you?" The thief winked, he didn't reply to the questions.

"It's best Oi move to 'nother compartment. Two doors is easier to get out of than one." He disappeared along the corridor.

The train drew slowly in to Havant station. Jon looked outside, preparing for a jump, but to his surprise he saw a train already in the other platform, the London train.

This is too good to be true. Wow, this could be dangerous. What would happen if the London train started as I was midway between the two trains. What if I couldn't open the London train door in time? Here goes, it's now or never.

He didn't hesitate. He opened his carriage door, climbed sideways on the step and managed to close it again without too much of a bang. Then with a leap which was creditable for a man of his age he landed on the up-train step and grabbed a door handle. Getting his balance he again lent sideways and opened the door, and climbed into the carriage with as much aplomb as he could, his bag bumping against his back. There was only one middle-aged passenger, and he was deep into the Times. He did not even raise his head when Jon appeared through the unaccustomed door.

Luck's in, now I must tidy up a bit. Wonder if the thief made it. Hope not, in a way. Don't want too much of his company. Glad that no ticket collectors come along the train. All tickets are shown at the barrier. Must solve the problem of getting through the barrier when I get there. My, I feel sleepy again. It's so stuffy.

He drifted into a light sleep. The train made one more stop, but no one came into his compartment, it was too early for the commuter passengers. He was woken by a nudge.

"'Ullo Guv. Had a good sleep? Sorry to disturb yer."

"You are not at bit sorry," laughed Jon, "otherwise you wouldn't have come in. Had any trouble?"

"Just a bit," replied the thief, grinning hugely. "The compartment Oi got into was first class. Two blokes thought Oi'd come from outer space. Thought they were going to kick up a stink. Walked straight passed with me 'ead up, took no notice of 'em, Oi didn't. Spent the rest of the journey in the damn toilets. 'Til jest now, that is."

On arrival at Victoria it was hard for Jon to shrug off the thief and go his own way. "Best we go through the barriers by ourselves, don't you think?" he asked hoping the thief would agree. Jon approached the barrier, fiddling in his pocket as he did so. Eye signals flashed between the ticket collector and himself, and there were no questions. Jon was allowed through the barrier.

Must be some sort of bush telegraph with these men here. Seem to be getting preferential treatment. Thank God for that. Those three men round the fire must have done their spade work. Great Scott, you still here? Why are you walking so close behind me, exactly in my footsteps?

Jon felt a tinge of annoyance. The thief only winked. "Can't help yer with the tea, Guv, told yer Oi were skint. Got any money?"

"Enough for a cuppa," said Jon. "A cuppa and a fag." Jon passed down the counter of the station restaurant and bought two cups of tea and a packet of cigarettes. He did not have much money left over. The thief was smirking as he stuck as close to Jon as he could, and he over sincerely gushed his thanks for the tea and the smoke.

"Bet yer could do with a sandwich, Guv," asked the thief.

"Or a pie," said Jon wishfully.

"Well then, 'ere's both," and with great alacrity the little man produced from the inside pocket of his coat an unbelievable assortment of food he had lifted on the way through the self-service counter. Jon roared with laughter, bordering on the insane. The thief had utter disregard of his personal safety as with great aplomb he proudly presented his last surprise, two doughnuts. Jon felt like a new boy in terms of self-sufficiency, and knew that he had a great deal to learn. His propriety was toyed with by this juggler of convention, and their relationship violated all the reasons for which he was 'outside', but all he did was to offer the thief yet another cigarette. Jon wondered what would have happened to him if the authorities had seen him with the thief when the meal was rifled. He already felt he was on the police's black-list, his roaming ways, his clothes, his speaking in the Park, his bouts of minor disorder when drunk, all made him a target for them. It would have been difficult for him to prove his innocence, and he would be easy meat for a copper who wanted to add some names to his list of charges, much easier than catching an active burglar who needed physical and mental effort to make the charge.

"O.K. for today, Guv? Be seein' yer."

"Take care of yourself," was all Jon could say before the thief silently melted into the background.

CHAPTER FOUR

Here, There and Everywhere

Leaving Victoria Station behind him, Jon pottered down Warwick Street and into Birdcage Walk and so to St. James's Park. He turned into the small hut serving as the public toilet at the end of the lake. Ablutions performed he felt more ready to face the task ahead. It was already rising 7.30am, and Jon knew he would be late for work.

Damn good thing too. That stupid twerp of a superintendent will get all worked up. I'll just tell him I'll work today, then he can give me my money, and I'm off. It's sad about Kate, maybe upset her a bit. She's happier now, so I don't mind so much. Think she'll understand.

He walked up Shaftesbury avenue, and climbed the stairs to the fourth floor in the Lyons building, so putting off his encounter for a few extra minutes. The storm soon broke. Before Jon had taken off his coat and hung up his cap, the superintendent swept into the cloakroom.

"You're fired," he said. "You're fired. An hour late and looking like a scarecrow! What will all the youngsters think? You've been trouble since you arrived. First you suck up, then you become familiar with the junior staff. Too clever by half, you think you are. Never been able to pin anything on you. And now I have. Thank goodness for that. Here's your wages for the morning, and I don't want to see you again." Jon said nothing, but looked the angry man straight in the eye. This seemed to aggravate the superintendent even further. He started on another spiel, holding the envelope with the money in his hand.

"I'll take my money." Jon interrupted, and in a very quiet voice he continued, "I've done nothing wrong until today. Remember that. I have never caused these people one moment's unease. We have all laughed together and enjoyed each other. I have always tried to make people feel good about themselves." The superintendent flinched, but said nothing. "I have never once made them feel threatened or provoked. Can you say the same about yourself?" Jon took the envelope, turned on his heel, and with cap in his hand and coat on his arm he walked off down the stairs. Back in St. James's Park he took stock of his situation.

I've got two pounds and some coppers, adequate clothing for a while, fifteen fags, and no more money coming in as things stand. It's getting colder and colder, and the days are shorter and shorter. I must get another job. It's Monday today, and I must speak again next Sunday. Got to go on meeting people. Got to convince them of the dangers around. Hyde Park is the best place for that. I hope to God I'm doing enough. There's often a glimmer of hope in some people's eyes when I've had a chat with them. Now... must think about work, and where I can go. Beginning to look real scruffy, I am, though I'm pretty clean. Clothes could do with an iron, and my shoes are down at heel. 'Spose that's one sign of a vagrant. Must try my hand at the hospitals. Somewhere where they're not too fussy about asking for an address. Could always give Trevor's flat, but that's giving me an advantage others haven't got. It's getting more and more difficult to get work without an address, same as you can't get Social Security at all without a base. Funny place, this park, I'm feeling it belongs to me. It's lovely here when the sun shines. Feel happy just sitting here. Not so much movement as there is in Hyde Park. Feel this place is my private garden. The pubs are my night time sitting room, and the rolling stock my bedroom. Perhaps soon it will be boxes, and boxes and boxes, cardboard, plastic, anything. I'll try my hand at one of the hospitals on the south bank.

Nothing ventured, nothing gained, and it's a new area. Haven't been around there much, and maybe the cops won't know me. It's a beautiful walk, anyway, over the bridge.

He walked slowly down to Horseferry Road and came to Lambeth Bridge. Here he stayed awhile on the bridge, watching the tugs pushing their long barges up and down stream. He saw the passenger boats, and the pleasure boats, and as it was high tide there were two little sailing boats having a race with each other.

Every man to himself, hope they have fun. I'm a landlubber myself. It all looks so busy, yet so tranquil. Water seems to slow people down to the pace of nature, 'cept for the damned competitive speed boats. Again money buying power. What's the point of just going fast from A to B when there's nothing to do at B when you arrive there? Still I'm wasting time letting my mind potter around like this. Wish I could have a vacuum in my head for a moment to let bits of poetry come popping in. Just surviving takes such a lot of effort.

He lit another cigarette, but with the chill air blowing off the river he felt he could dawdle no longer and he got himself started on the last bit of the journey.

Jon arrived at the hospital, and looked up at the large building, some of it still shrouded in tarpaulins. The place seemed to be having a face lift and an added extension. He waited in the street outside the gates to watch those going in and out. A sprinkling of nurses walked hurriedly by, cloaks wrapped well around, all talking together animatedly as if oblivious to the traumas going on inside. The old walked by slowly, resignation written across their faces, and the young mothers dragged reluctant children towards the entrance. He noticed a white faced small boy tugging at his mother's hand.

"Come on, Mum, it's got to be done. I'll be better when it's over." Jon looked closely at the determined small figure, and the harassed and fearful expression of his mother. Under his pom-pom hat the little chap was bald. Jon knew what he was going to have done to him, more treatment for cancer. The mother looked fleetingly at Jon as if appealing for help.

"You've a fine lad there," said Jon to the woman. "Wish there were more about like him." When the woman smiled her face lit up. "What do you want to be when you grow up? Bet you've thought all about that?" he asked the boy, hoping a chat would give the woman time to collect herself.

"I'm going to be a footballer. Play in goal for England. But I've got to get better first. Mum's scared. I'm not. It's quite fun in there with all the others. Come on, Mum, don't be scared."

"Make sure you get tickets when he gets his first cap, won't you?" The woman laughed at Jon's remark.

"He's a tough little nut," she said. "I'm the stupid one, get all bothered and frightened. 'Spose it's because I'm his mum. Bit special he is to me."

"He's a bit special to everyone, don't you think? Bit special to the doctors and nurses? They'll look after him." Jon saw the boy pulling at his mother's arms. Then Jon added, looking directly at the mother, "Now you go first and take him in. Show him how brave YOU are, that'll make things easier for him."

"Bye now, and thanks. I'll be O.K." the woman said and turned for the hospital, holding the boy's hand she led him quickly to the door. After a few moments Jon followed them in, and went up to the Reception desk. He was starting to feel tired, so he cracked no jokes, simply asked to be directed to the Personnel Department explaining that he was looking for part time employment. He was given directions, and found himself walking down a long high corridor.

Don't really fit in here. Everyone sees to know what they want and where they are going, they're all in such a hurry. 'Spect most people have what they want and are getting where they want to go. Couldn't half do with a sit down and a pint. My feet are killing me, burning and throbbing. Don't think this is the right place for me.

He soon found the sign saying "Administration." He knocked at the door, and heard a voice calling him in. He stood at the first desk. A young girl was typing, and took no notice of him.

"Excuse me, a voice told me to come in. Here I am. What do you expect me to do?" Jon was getting ruffled.

Without looking from her machine, the young girl called, "Audrey, customer. Can you come, please?" Still standing, Jon waited a few more moments till an elderly lady well loaded with bosom came from behind a partition.

"What can I do for you? What is it that you want?" she asked sharply.

"What I don't want is to have to stand up much longer." Jon said cheekily. The woman looked Jon up and down. "I came looking for a part time job. I've always given good service, but somehow I don't think I'm being made to feel welcome."

"We don't take people just off the streets," said the woman coldly. "We only take applicants with references, or from the Unemployment Exchange. I have work available, but I'm sure you're not suited to it. Good-day."

"Good-day to you, madam. And I'm sure I don't wish to be in a place where appearances are first priority, and rudeness is the order of the day. Perhaps you'll come to find out that people are valuable, and that it is possible to work well even in an old coat. Goodbye, madam, and when you mirror your thoughts I hope you're pleased with the result." He turned and walked out of the room, leaving the stout woman looking dumbfounded.

Stupid old bitch, she looked as if she never laughed in her life. I knew I'd cooked my goose when I started to be cheeky.

It was well passed midday and Jon knew from experience that he would not find work easily in the afternoon. He walked slowly towards Waterloo Station, hunger pains making his stomach rumble and tiredness weaving through his limbs. His back ached, and his head swam. His right foot was very cold. He bent to look at his shoe, and saw that he had walked right through the sole and his sock was wet.

No wonder my feet are cold. Top priority a pair of boots. Next priority something to drink, hot if possible. Then somewhere warm for the night. Don't know about food. Don't even feel like alcohol. I'm just bloody exhausted.

He walked on slowly, and came to lower Marsh Street, and a small group of shops. He saw the oldest second hand junk shop he had seen for a long time, and looked into the window. He opened the door and a bell jangled in the back premises, a bell that was attached to the door by a string. He smelt stale leather, dust, old books and rust.

Not likely to find boots here. But some odd feeling told me to come in, so I must just chance it. Can't see much the light's so poor. Windows are so dirty, and cobwebs all over the place. Ah ha! Someone's coming. Goodness me, I've not seen such a shrivelled old man for ages. He seems like Methuselah. How does he make a living out of a place like this?

"Arternoon, sir, what can I do for you?" The old man spoke in a cracked high-pitched voice. He kept on adjusting his tiny round gold rimmed spectacles. His hair stood out in tufts all over his head and badly needed a brush.

"Afternoon. That's a better welcome than the one I've just had from the staff in the hospital. I came for some boots, but I don't see any." Jon looked all around. "Good thick boots like the ones I had in the army. I don't expect you've any tucked away?"

"Bin in the army, have you? I remember the first war. Right old time that was. Lucky to come out with my wits and my limbs. Too old for the second war." While the quaint little man was talking he was rummaging in a box behind an old table that served as a counter. "Just got these two pairs. Size 9 and 10. Not quite new, but they're strong. Better than the rubbish about nowadays."

"I've only got a pound," said Jon, taking the larger size of boots. "May I try them on?" He sat on a wobbly chair, and tried on the boots and they fitted well. The junk man sat on a box opposite. He accepted the pound without comment. He seemed in no hurry, and anxious to talk. Jon kept the boots on. He offered the old man a cigarette, and they started to talk. Jon watched the evening light creep into darkness, and still the old man talked, and Jon was fascinated, and he listened quietly, his hunger and tiredness forgotten. The moon was high in the sky when the old man let Jon out into the street.

"That was real nice. My name's Herbert, and you're welcome to come whenever you like. Don't get the chance of a good talk. Young 'uns, and the not so young, are all in a rush. Can't be bothered with an old 'un. Come again, come again." They shook hands and Jon walked on towards Waterloo station.

Life deals good cards at unexpected moments, must leave yourself open. Don't put limits on life. Must follow inner consciousness and all will be well. Old Herbert's a good man, he is: had a positive way of thinking in spite of all his hard times. Maybe I'll visit him again, but I don't want to get beholden. And now for a cuppa, a well earned cuppa.

He turned into Waterloo station and headed for the tea wagon where everything was cheaper than in the main restaurant. With his remaining pound he bought tea and two sandwiches, and sat on a bench to eat them, making them last as long as possible. After an hour's rest he felt better, and knew it was time to move on. He had already seen the station police walk by twice and they looked at him with unsmiling eyes.

He spent time in the toilets, making use of the hot water. He was even able to wash his feet and managed a splash around his groin when there was nobody there. He walked away from the entrance along the length of the platform where a uniformed body was piling up the mail bags.

"Evening mate," said Jon, trying to sum the fellow up.

"Hi," came the reply. "Wanting something?"

Jon put his cards on the table. "I'm desperate for a sleep. Got some friends in Victoria who tip me the wink where I can get a kip. Any ideas?"

"I've heard about you. Anything unusual travels fast amongst us. They seem to think you're a good guy, with lots to say." The worker looked all round him. There was no one about.

"Waiting to be cleaned, platform 12. But don't say I said." The man got on with stacking the mail bags.

Jon was on platform 6. That meant he had six platforms to cross. "Thanks, mate. Good of you to understand," and he disappeared into the shadows to make his plan. Suddenly memories flooded his mind.

Hell, being on a station like this evading authority is bringing back bad, bad memories. Poor old Chalky. He was a good mate to have as a p.o.w. Those four nights and days we spent on the top of a goods van hiding under a tarpaulin when we had slipped camp! Glad that didn't happen again. Chocolate and rainwater wasn't much to keep us going all that time. Fancy not knowing where we were going. Train was heading west, and that's all we could gather. No names on the stations didn't help. And what a huge railway station we ended up in, twice as big as this. Dense fog too, but Chalky was determined to jump and run. Bloody stupid, we couldn't see our hands in front of our faces the fog was so bad. The tracks were like a spider's web, and we couldn't tell if we were between the tracks or in the path of the trains which had no lights. Just rumbled at us they did. One of the worst times of my life. Terrible to feel so helpless. No wonder we were caught, stumbling about like drunkards. At least I am not in a foreign country, though sometimes I feel this one is just as alien. At least I'm not between the tracks with the trains rumbling by, and I'm not frightened or helpless. I've only got myself to fend for. I think I'll cross the line on this curve, no one should see me. Darned noise these new boots make. Off they come. Now I really look like a crook.

He chuckled to himself. Without misadventure he reached Platform 12, found the train, and a first class carriage. He put his boots on again in case he had to make a quick get away, and lay down for his longed for sleep. The train was not heated so he was cold and shivery, but he closed his eyes and was soon in dreamland. He was woken by a sloshing noise outside and realised that the windows were being cleaned. He lay low and still, knowing that he could not be seen from ground level.

Well, I'm really a lucky old bugger. I've got two allies for my hotel on wheels. Just got to dodge the uniformed dosser catchers. Must get off these premises as quickly as possible, and start this soul destroying job hunting. That's most urgent. And I must tow the line for a while. Too much hassle and too many changes of jobs will stop me from speaking in the Park and meeting people.

After some difficulty Jon found more work in another pub in a small street off the Strand. He ate that evening for the first time that day, and received the balance of his pay that night. This pub did not provide free meals, but he was allowed a much reduced rate. When Jon arrived in the Park on the following Sunday, he found a larger crowd than usual waiting around in spite of the cold wind and wintry conditions. He was glad of his strong boots, and thick coat. He chatted as usual to several of the crowd, a motley lot, with a few tourists and the more affluent. Then he found his box, stood on it and started to speak.

"Today I'm going to speak just as an individual, speaking to and for you, or anyone, as an individual. It's difficult just to be an individual, with your own thoughts, your own opinions, your own way of doing things."

"'eard this all before. Yer sed this before."

"I've said something on these lines," Jon replied to the voice. Then he turned his head to address the larger numbers. "It's so much easier to move with the mob, think as a mob, do nothing to challenge authority or convention. Is that how some of you feel?" There were a few nods from the crowd.

"Sure, and why not? Why bring notice to yourself?" a younger voice asked.

Jon continued not wanting his flow of thought to be diverted. "Anyone who stands out against authority is marked by that authority. Anyone who speaks out for the individual is on hostile ground anywhere in the world. What about the individual who is poor? Who speaks out for them? Or for groups of poor people, or for whole countries of poor people? No political party anywhere wants poor people. They present too much of a problem just because of numbers, the numbers of the poor are so great."

"Go on wiv yer," shouted another irate man. "We've 'eard all this before. Thought yer were goin' to give us somethin' diff'rent. That's the kind of crap the Christians give us, or the Buddhists, or the Communists. What 'bout 'em Conservatives? Sitting on their backsides all day, loaded in 'em pockets, tellin' us 'ow to live. It's wot religionists and all politicians 'ave told us since we got out of 'em caves."

Jon let the man rant on. Finally the man's anger died down, and he finished by saying in a quieter tone, "Give us 'ope, man, give us 'ope. Somethin' that each one of these systems don't give us. 'Ope, that's what we want."

"Words are too cheap for that remark," replied Jon.

"Then why do you use words?" asked the same irate man.

"I'll tell you why. I use words to tell you that you are not alone in society's rejection of the likes of us, the so-called poor. It may appear contradictory to say you can share aloneness. But it is true in our circumstances and can be done. In this truth we can build bridges to one another by acts, not acts of violence which are shown as the bonfires of war burn throughout the world, but by loving person to person acts, moment by moment. Jon paused, the crowd was silent. "The only qualification for this is to see the need in each individual that we meet, and act to try and fill that need. The more we fill these needs by deeds the stronger we will become through each experience, and with discipline and respect of the other person we will find a growth of love." Jon saw the irate man starting to grumble again. "Oh, I know that you are going to say that there is nothing new in all that, as our friend the black clothed priest over there has just said," he pointed to a minister who gesticulated wildly. "All I have said is covered by the philosophies wilting under the strain as our planet lurches towards the twenty-first century. But I would like to make you aware of a hope that cannot be touched by man made manipulations. You all have life, this you know, your own senses tell you that. We all have life, an inner life, that no one from the outside can touch."

"Inner life, outer life. Don't accept that crap." Leading his woman by the arm a middle-aged spectator pushed his way from the front of the crowd.

"Pity he didn't stay," Jon commented. "He just might have picked up some good feelings. I'll finish soon... I want you all to feel stronger for having heard my words.... When we have met other peoples' 'need' by 'deed', then our senses are able to strengthen our grip on our inner lives. Don't forget about this inner part of yourself. When that inner part of you starts to feel strong you will have hope."

"Sorry mate, it's all a bit too much..." and with this comment the crowd, showing their boredom, started to drift away.

Pity. All they seem to want is fire and brimstone that they can go on grumbling against. Anything resembling the truth about themselves they shy away from. I'm not going to betray my principles just to hold their attention. I must say what I feel is right. That's why I'm here.

There was one person left. She was a young American girl, red lipped and red nailed, wearing a warm furry coat and real leather boots and bag. She waited till everyone had gone, then she spoke.

"I liked what you said. I'd like to be able to help." She looked embarrassed as she put her hand into her bag and pulled out a wallet stuffed with notes. "Can you accept this? It may be able to help you help others. Go on keeping your concern for others in the forefront of your mind and deeds."

Are you trying to buy me? What do you want of me? Hell, I musn't think things like that till I have proof. You don't look devious to me, just desperately anxious that I have the money. Don't think you've an ulterior motive. I can't accept the money. I'd be in her debt and she might manipulate me. Oh dear, suspicious still. I must be a fool to refuse it. Think of all the pints and cups of tea it would buy and still leave plenty for other people.... 'Fraid she must find some other way to help people.

"Believe me," said Jon gently, "I'm truly sorry, but I cannot accept the money." He gave no reason, and was sad to see the girl flush. He would have liked to ask her why she wanted to part with what appeared a large amount, but she turned and walked away, her head bowed. Jon walked to the restaurant on the lake and had two teas and toast. He moved to a quiet corner on the balcony under a light, thankful that he did not have to work on the Sunday night shift at the pub. The wintry sun shone defiantly through the bare trees making a tracery of twigs and branches against the sky. Jon felt at peace with himself again, yet concerned at the apparent inability of the man in the crowd to understand what he was saying. He took his pad and pen, and this is what he wrote.

Laugh not except at the skimming surface of my hopes. I would seek to offer no insult to your imagination. If for any reason I cannot be understood, then accept my sincerity, try to find a meeting point of reciprocated tolerance. Just out of curiosity do not plumb the depths of reason. If there is a residue of good in whatever I seek for others, emerge encouraged, follow the goodness, guarding progress and enjoy each precious improvement. Support those who seek this most radical of changes ever demanded. Without fear bring the impossible into the more understandable areas of the improbable so that hope continues to emerge. Let all movements forward be accompanied with poise and calm and in doing so part of humanities great great need will be met. True power, sometimes hidden, does not oppose beauty and joy, nor does it wish to shorten the journey of life. But beware! Watch unless the sense of haste should misjudge expedience and in so doing make stagnant violence, erupt with destruction's devastating force.

He sighed, and put the pad back into his pocket. The shutters were going up in the cafe so Jon knew he should be moving on. As he was already in the Park he decided to doss amongst the trees or bushes, anywhere where he could not be seen. He rummaged in the bins surrounding the cafe, and found several bags of assorted sizes which he needed for warmth and to keep him dry. Then he crossed the main path, taking care there was no one about, and disappeared into the shrubs. He relieved himself again, and then began to bed down, one bag for each foot and the rest underneath his body. It was very cold, first one leg cramped, then the foot on the other side, and pain screeched the length of his lower limbs. His fingers started to numb: he was too cold to shiver. The night passed very slowly.

Chapter Five

Colder and Colder

Jon woke after a disturbed night when the birds began their dawn chorus. He lay still, too cold to move his stiff and painful limbs. The frost had made crystals on his beard and eyebrows.

God, I'm cold. Cold right through to the marrow. Ow, that pain! When I move my legs it's terrible. But it's not as bad as when I was on the run in Poland, so I know I can cope. Just got to get the circulation going, got to get moving. Can't let myself freeze up like this. The taste in my mouth. Ugh! Clear up these bags, then I'm off. Twice round the Park then a cuppa. Must think about smoking. Got to stop it. Waste of money, and doing my lungs no good.

He walked round the Park once, and then at the beginning of the second round, near Rotten Row, he saw a familiar figure.

I'll be damned if that isn't old Rod. Used the same commuter train as I did. Wonder if he'll see me, and if he sees me wonder if he'll acknowledge me. My beard's grown a bit, and haven't got a collar and tie. Bet the old bastard has recognised me. Not going to let him get away with it this time.

The two men walked towards each other. Rodney, well dressed in camel hair coat and trilby, looked at Jon, and quickly looked away again.

"Hi, Rodney, 7.55 still the same as ever?"

"Well, well," Rodney feigned surprise. "Fancy meeting you here. Didn't recognise you."

"Fib number one," Jon chided. "You didn't want to recognise me. Right?"

Rodney nodded. As if to make up for his double-think he said, "I've got half an hour, come and have a cuppa and tell me about everything."

"Suits me," said Jon, and they went to the lakeside restaurant which had just opened for breakfasts. Two teas were ordered, and Jon, hungry as he was, did not ask for toast or anything else to eat.

When tea was brought, Rodney offered Jon a cigarette. "No thanks," said Jon. "Must give it up. Bad for the blood and bad for the circulation. I've promised myself I'll stop it, and I'm damn well going to. It's mighty tempting though, seeing you puff away."

"My, you have changed. What's it all about? Where are you living? What are you doing? Can't say you look good. In fact you look awful." Rodney looked around at the incoming visitors.

"Ashamed to be seen with me?" challenged Jon. "A few clothes don't change what's inside. You've known me for years. But it's like so many people I meet. They look away. My old friends don't seem to be able to accept me like this. They put it down to my eccentricity, which after all is a polite way of saying I am mad."

"What **has** made this difference to you? Why are you taxing yourself like this, you're no longer a young man. You look as if you could do with a jolly good scrub."

Jon didn't answer the questions, but he shot a severe look at Rodney. "Privacy and its invasion is something to be studied." Then in a gentler voice he continued, "it appears that the social stigma against being a dosser makes even a burglar look respectable. The thief catcher, either in or out of uniform, dislikes the physical appearance of the dosser, but the only crime a dosser commits is against himself, being a down and out. The thief can live, either in the Ritz or at Wormwood Scrubs, but rarely has he no fixed abode. A high proportion of the antagonism against the Wino dosser trap is based on his physical appearance and his non-conformity, and this gives the harassment factor fuller licence and opportunity."

"You haven't changed much, Jon. Always been on the side of the under-dog, haven't you? But I must admit I feel embarrassed when I pass a dosser. Feel I should give him some cash, yet then I feel I might hurt his feelings."

Jon replied obliquely, "the reason for the beggar being there is not an elegant affair, but it helps to see that other men are made aware of what one yardstick of failure can mean in a material worshipping world."

"Still dabbling in the poetical world?" queried Rodney who then steered the conversation to more mundane matters; he was ill at ease with his situation. Looking at his watch he said, "Must off now," and he stretched for his hat and coat. "Any messages?" and he looked at Jon with questioning eyes.

"No specific messages," replied Jon understanding the unspoken question. "Just tell them in Weybridge that I'm well and still trying to head in the right direction." The two men separated, each to go their own way, a world of difference apart.

That week Jon kept a low profile at the pub, worked hard and ate as much as he could, even scraping the saucepans before they were cleaned.

It's not food I need so much, but sleep. Sleep and warmth. giving up smoking is not as hard as I thought, but I could never give up my tea and beer. Bad nights they were last week at Victoria. Got booked three times by railway police, the buggers, so I had little rest. Must find a new circle of movement. Don't want to get my accomplices into trouble.

In the middle of the week and when at work Jon saw

a young man drinking heavily. Under the pretext of clearing his table Jon asked quietly, "what's up? Looks as if you're trying to escape."

"I am that," replied the young man.

"Like to meet me at the door at 11 p.m? Got to work till then." Jon felt the young man could do with some attention, that he had needs which were causing a vacuum that drink was supposed to fill.

"O.K. I'll be there. Bit pissed, I 'xpect."

The youngster was waiting at the appointed time, a pillar propped him up.

"What's got you in this state?" asked Jon, taking him by the arm and leading him firmly towards St. James's Park. The cold night air had a sobering effect. The youngster was soon talking rationally.

"I've been teaching at the L.S.E. for a year. Can't make them out. They arrive full of enthusiasm, just kids they are, and within a year they've changed. They become cynical, coarse, sometimes dirty, and I'm sure many are on drugs. I can see it in their eyes, pupils all dilated, but I've never caught them at it. Feel I should be able to do something, but they just mock me."

"Steady now, young man," said Jon. "Let's sit here, it's out of the wind, and won't be too cold."

"It's so difficult," the young man interrupted. "If you leave things then it comes too late so..."

Comfortably seated between a tree and a hut Jon continued, "don't try to take on the world. You're aware of what is happening. Be yourself, and bide your time. Youth becomes an early victim in the present system's conversion of teenagers to be a materialistic consumer, they can't resist the pressures. There's a carrot and stick persuasion method of breaking in the unwilling youngster to submit to the competitive circle of activity which then absorbs 60% of his working life. The only consolations for doing what he's not cut out to do is the creaking bed and the fear of failure, and not being able to keep up his payments on his hire purchase."

"What a future, poor young sods." The young man shook his head.

"I find this Government completely without awareness." Jon looked at the youngster for his reactions. There were none. "The last year of school should be termed "Lifemanship", and should be geared to build up enthusiasm, optimism, and awareness."

"That's Utopian" murmured the listener.

"They should be taught how to make compromises, and have their personal motives checked and guided. Lifemanship and comradeship should be equated in the examinations. They should be shown how society cares for them, and what society expects of them. There should be a sophisticated appraisal devoid of acidity."

"That would be a dream world," sighed the young man. "But thanks for talking. I don't think I'll wallow in self pity and beer again. Pointless, isn't it? My, I'm cold.... Must be off. Thanks for giving me your time and talking to me.... I've a flat in Kensington. Bit of a walk. Never mind. Sure you're O.K? Bye and thanks again." Unconcerned for Jon's situation he didn't wait for an answer, Jon wouldn't have given him one anyway. The youngster walked off into the darkness, leaving Jon on the bench. The moment of communication had quickly arisen, and equally quickly evaporated. It was midnight: again the chill air sent warning messages.

Can't doss down just yet. Too many people about. Will leg it to Euston and try there. Big enough place, but it's new, and I'm not sure of the lay-out. Walking will get me warm. Mighty tired I am. Sleep, sleep, glorious sleep. Why are you so hard to find?

Halfway down Marylebone High Street Jon passed a figure slouched against a lamp post. It was another old man and he looked blue with cold, and his eyes were clouded and blank. Jon handed him what he thought were two pennies. The man spat at him. Jon took no notice and went on walking.

Poor old buffer. He's losing control. Wonder what's got him to that state. It makes me sick and sad to see another human being losing his dignity. Must get a cuppa before I turn in, warm myself up a bit. Shouldn't have had that big meal and all that beer. Left me a bit short of cash. Lets see what I've left. Should still have two half crowns. What only pennies? Damn and blast. Must have given the silver to that sodder. And it produced a spit. No tea for me and nothing till tomorrow evening. Cheerful thought! Ah, here's Euston. Perhaps I can take the weight off my poor legs. Bugger of buggers, there's the station police van. Can't go there now. Must find somewhere else. God I'm tired.

With an aching body and throbbing head and feet that were swelling up, and a dirty tasting mouth he walked back towards Regent's Park. He came to Park Square Gardens, and saw a gap in the fence. Too tired to look around to see if there was anybody about, he squeezed through the gap, found the nearest and thickest bush, and lay down under it in the foetus position, even too tired to bother with the plastic bags. He was woken with the clatter of milk bottles. The silent electric milk float was on its morning rounds. Cold and stiff and sore Jon squeezed back through the hole in the fence. Dawn was just breaking, there was no one about except the milk man.

Jon approached the milk float slowly, his legs were so cold that they would not go fast, he could not feel his toes.

"Hi, mate. Bit cold it was last night. Any spares with tops off? My mouth's like a bird cage."

"Yer luck's in. Tits been at the side crates when I was delivering. Takes time to climb some of 'em stairs. Can't do two at a time now. Broken gold top there. Plenty with silver tops all pecked at. Take yer pick."

"You're a godsend," said Jon warmly, gripping the gold top and one of the silver tops. "But my fingers are so cold I can hardly hold them."

"'Ere yer are, bud. 'Ave a bag. Think I've got some of yesterday's bread too. Any good to yer? Don't like to see a cold 'un. You'd better look arter yerself. Not as young as you used to be, eh? Much best you ask me than nicking bottles off doorsteps. That gets me into trouble."

"Never nicked a pint, and I don't intend to. Thanks a lot. Maybe see you again."

With the bread and milk clutched to his chest, Jon hobbled to Regents Park. He found the public toilets open, and to his joy he found a hot pipe running round near the floor. He knelt to warm first his hands, then his legs and finally he took off his boots and warmed his feet.

Hope I can get the boots on again. Feet are getting very bad. Much too swollen for this time of day. God, it hurts as they get warm. Hope nobody comes in. I'll look a right banana with my boots off. Must wash out a few things when I get to the pub tonight. I've found an airing cupboard, and don't think they'll be spotted. This is a blooming feast. Milk AND bread. Thought I'd get nothing all day. Another unexpected card of good fortune dealt out to me. With all this effort to keep going I may not last too long. May get sick. How do the other poor buggers in their boxes survive? They don't do much all the time like I do. Just live from day to day with little hope for a better tomorrow. What is the alternative to survival for them? Living on the brink of the alternative, no wonder they feel a sense of hopelessness and helplessness. I want more out of life, both for me and for the unborn. That's what keeps me going.

It had taken Jon over half and hour to thaw out. He used the toilet facilities and had as good a wash as possible, then propped himself against the wash basin and slowly ate half the bread and drank one bottle of milk. The rest he kept for later. A new day had begun.

The following Sunday the crowds were larger than ever. Jon looked around and saw two faces that he recognised, the little thief and the irate man of the previous session. He was also glad to see a group of men of various ages who were obviously of the collar and tie brigade. He spotted some poker faced thugs, their only moving part was their eyes.

Got some minders there. Wonder who they are going to report back to? Not to worry, I'm going to talk in the only way I know. I'm not going to change my kind of approach. People will just have to pick up what I'm saying as well as they can. But I'll try for a bit more punch. Maybe do them good to have to use their brains a little.

Jon stood up on a step-ladder that he borrowed for a small agreed fee on tick from the nearby park keeper. He felt he could view the crowd better from higher up.

"Today I am going to tell you all how I feel the situation is at the moment, nothing to do with pounds, shillings and pence, or unions, or party politics. From time to time I will ask questions, but I do not want you to give me the answer, just think about the questions." He waited a moment.

"Can't see you've much left to talk about," said a voice. "If you're on to religion, then I'm off." The crowd did not heed the interruption and grew quiet.

Jon continued. "I lived in an age when people lost sight of liberty, and when they came to their senses they realised it had been removed. Whenever truth was approached, goodness and sanity were encircled. Those who tried to mitigate human hurt came up against hostility, everything became politics, party politics."

"Grow up, man. You should know by now everything is led by politics or leads to politics," the same voice called out again.

Jon disregarded the comment. "Words, words, words, all

fed to lonely people, which when consumed reduced the individual down to a mere number. Those who lived by all these words showed contempt for the deeds done by good people in everyday life. Innocence was made to look suspect, psychological pressures flooded in in camouflaged ways. Whatever they, the religious leaders, the politicians, the civil authorities, believed in was constantly foisted on the citizen of this land, and the citizen was expected to conform. Can you remember how often this has happened to you?"

"Sure, sure. You're right there. Got a point, you have." Jon heard these words from the edge of the crowd as he warmed to his subject.

"Those in authority lived differently from what they preached. Humanity was being led without the symbols of truth. Ask yourselves how many times you have felt facts have been manipulated to fit expediency." Jon paused.

"Go on, man. Go on." There were a few puzzled looks on nearby faces.

"In the name of this expediency, soul pollution has been encouraged, the right of the unborn ignored as the inventiveness of evil made all past misfortunes but a product of ignorance rather than of knowing. Never have the hopes of mankind been so mindlessly squandered, in spite of individuals trying to practice decency, trying to cultivate beauty, art and sensitivity into their life styles. Is it too late to apportion blame?"

"You tell us. That's what we've come to 'ear." Jon recognised the voice of the irate man of previous sessions.

"It is better that we seek gradual improvement rather than become off-balance to scale perfection's heights. Good ideals are the only way to that high standard, but that way is hard, sensitive. We should recognise that this journey to perfection needs some compromise, and no one is perfect, and while we should never condone retrograde confrontation between human beings, we should acknowledge the efforts of triers."

"Blimey, gettin' a bit 'igh an mighty, aren't you?" Another voice added excitement to the occasion.

"Confrontation does not produce the results which humanity needs, it only takes care of his wants, and that very poorly. The obstacles arising at the oncoming of the twenty-first century are many, and though there appears ever worsening dilemmas there is still hope within the individual, deep within. With this hope and with compassionate skill unity will return and the welfare of the individual will be enhanced." He looked around to see how the crowd were reacting.

"There will be no need to ask, as people in this great land of ours now ask, on which side of this human daily war is the law?" He paused again. The irate man was looking baffled, the thief did the victory sign with his two fingers, and the group of educated gentlemen were rubbing their chins, nodding, and smiling. The minders looked angry.

"What does survival mean?" Jon continued. "If, in the uncontrolled momentum impelled by wants, human dignity is thrown to the wind, and if uniformity curtails the spark of leadership, and if leadership by example is lost, where do we go from there?" He counted each 'if' on his fingers.

"Come off it man. You make me uneasy. Where DO we go?" It was the angry man again.

"In our time change will take place, and it will happen faster and at more cost than ever before. The cost may be more than each of us can freely give, but it may lead to living life without psychological hurt or living a defeat with suppression. If we can accept change at this pace, which mankind has never experienced before, mankind will have a rendezvous with destiny." Jon' voice crescendoed. "Preventative action will be able to offset collision's course, and reclaim 'NOW' with all its energies for a new era of survival with no preference and without casualties." He waited in the ensuing silence then stepped down from his ladder. It was a way of dismissing his audience. When he turned round he saw the crowd disappearing, the thief was waiting for his attention, and the silent men with angry eyes were still standing statue like.

"Well done, Guv. Mighty fine. If yer go on like this yer'll be asked to join them tha' sit in the 'ouse, tha' bloody great place by the river where them makes rules for us suckers."

"Somebody did drop me a hint the other day," laughed Jon. "But who in their right minds would support me looking as I do."

"Yer be alrigh', Guv. Be seeing yer. Oi'm keepin an eye on yer."

Jon understood the thief's good intentions, but he wished the law-breaker was not quite so liberal with his relationship within the view of the silent men. Jon knew they were the law in disguise and he knew that they were cognisant of the thief's misdoings. He was tired and hungry, so he boarded a train to try for a kip. That evening he persuaded the publican to let him do an extra Sunday shift for he needed a meal and the few shillings. It was midnight when he found himself back at Victoria.

He walked slowly across to the mobile tea bar. There were only a few people about, but the steady tread of the station police rhythmed in his head. Then disturbing events seemed to crescendo. Walking towards him came a female tramp, wispy hair sticking out under an old army beret, her long army coat trailing the ground. She carried two plastic bags. The only misdemeanour that Jon reasoned she could be doing was to walk very slowly. It looked as if her feet hurt. To his surprise he saw the two policemen turn and approach the tramp with quickened footsteps.

One took her arm, and roughly pointed her towards an Exit. "Out of here and quick," said the senior policeman. "I know the likes of you. You're not going to travel, so get out quick. Otherwise it will be the nick for you, for loitering." They gave the old woman a shove and she shuffled slowly towards the Exit. Jon felt anger well up inside him. She had committed no proven offence. He was about to interfere, but then he saw a well dressed woman approach the group.

Ah, now what will their attitude be? She might be a tart for all we know looking for new areas for her beat. Just look at her, sidling up to the policeman. Bet she'd have them in bed given half a chance.

"Evening, Officer," she said looking coyly at the older man, making her cleavage more evident by allowing her coat to open. "Do you think it's too late for me to get a taxi?"

"No, madam," said the policeman oilily, his eyes flickering towards her bosom. "I'm sure if you telephoned Enquiries and asked them for an all-night number you'd find one. Goodnight, madam, glad to be of help."

After smiling the woman had turned away. She never went towards a telephone booth.

"Couldn't leave the old girl with her dignity, could you? She hadn't committed an offence. For all you know she could have been going about her business, minding her own business". Jon angrily called after the police. "Just smarmed at the woman because of her cleavage. Couldn't you see she wanted to lay you?"

"Mind what you say. We've got our eyes on you, and the likes of you. You bugger off, or you'll be had for trespassing, let along loitering." The older man, a sergeant, puffed out his chest and looked aggressive.

"The trouble is," said Jon standing his ground, "that there is no one to protest to, no one who can say stop to brutal treatment of the individual, no one strong enough to say that this is a public concourse. I'll have you know I am contemplating taking a journey in the immediate future so do not molest me, or lay one finger on me. The only time when you have authority to do this is when I, by my actions, need restraining from hurting myself or others. As long as I have other people's welfare at heart I challenge you not to violate my dignity, and that applies to that old lady too."

"Piss off," said the sergeant, "I don't for one minute think you are planning a journey. There's only the 1.30 a.m. left to go. Just piss off and let us get on with the job." Jon turned and walked off. He trudged wearily to Oxford Circus, the only people about were other shadowy figures slowly moving in the same direction. Finally he spent the remains of the night with a group of louse-ridden, smelly and very drunken young people on the second level at Oxford Circus. They were not disturbed, and Jon snatched the sleep gratefully. He was glad he had nothing valuable to steal for in the morning he found his few remaining cigarettes had disappeared.

With the money saved from tobacco smoking he bought re-inforcements of warm wear from the little old man in the tiny shop who sold him the boots.

Never mind what I look like. With this odd cap and huge scarf I'll be more incognito than ever. Wonder where the fellow gets all this old stuff from. It's so cheap he can't make a living. Can just manage to keep clean and avoid smelling badly by using the toilet facilities whenever possible, specially the ones at the pub. Some dossers smell ghastly, poor chaps. They've got beyond caring. But it's an ongoing battle to keep my feet from getting blistered and ulcerated. Must watch out for them. Once an ulcer starts I'll never get rid of it. Glad they've given me that three quarter jacket to work in. Covers up a lot.

One early morning after a night spent in a cardboard box down an alley way in Soho, perched off the ground on two milk crates Jon was stretching his cold and aching limbs.

"Come on, Guv, hurry up." There was the thief, looking as perky as if he had slept on a feather bed. "Follow me, and do exactly as I say." Rather bemused, Jon followed the little man, hobbling painfully on his frozen feet. They proceeded to the staff quarters of the Allambra Hotel on

Park Lane, one of the biggest and most expensive hotels in London.

It was too early in the morning for the time-keeper to be wide awake. Guarding the staff entrance, he sat hunched up and half asleep. The thief, followed by Jon, moved in almost military style towards the time clock immediately opposite the office. The thief drew out a numbered card, clicked the time-clock bell without putting the card in and returned the card to the section from which he had taken it. Jon followed this procedure well enough. This first obstacle was over, and the thief continued to lead the way to the chef's changing room.

"Oi know my way around 'ere," he said. "Now put these on fast," and he extracted two complete sets of chef's clothing. "We've got just five minutes before the real chefs 'll be 'ere." He said that with a mischievous grin. Then he carried out a mock inspection of Jon's somewhat untidy appearance, adjusting Jon's clothing with the air of a bullying sergeant-major. Jon stayed silent.

"Yer'll 'ave to do," said the thief, "now, yer watch me. Watch me all the time." Jon followed the thief into the dining area, where they both helped themselves liberally to a mixed-grill breakfast, complete with porridge and the very much needed cup of tea. The flamboyance of the action of the thief was as though he had always worked there. His repartee with the staff, while not being familiar, seemed to confirm his role as a chef. Jon, less sure and with some trepidation, followed, and only relaxed when both chose a table away from the rest of the staff who were enjoying their breakfasts. They were soon tucking into a sumptuous meal.

"Now yer'll be feelin' be'er," said the thief. "Want another cup of tea? Put a cigarette into yer face till Oi gets back." Then he added in louder tones, "I've got a good mind to complain about this porridge. It's not as good as when I do it."

"Holy Moses," Jon muttered. "You've got a nerve." They

both chuckled. Jon fiddled with the cigarette but did not light up. The thief returned not with just two cups of tea but four.

"Och," he laughed, "it's no good having courage if yer don't use it. Look man, yer 'aven't lit up yet. Bad as that, is it?"

"Given it up," said Jon shortly. He was now completely thawed out after his night at Cardboard Hall, and he swigged the tea with a hurriedness that the thief abhorred.

"With such manners, I'm not sure I can take you anywhere," laughed the thief. Sustained by such a welcome meal they were warm both inside and out, and soon they were on the street again and well away from the hotel.

"Thanks, mate," said Jon, "now I feel I can breathe freely again, but you certainly have some cheek. Wouldn't have thought of that in a thousand years."

"See yer," waved the thief, and again he melted into his surroundings.

Adversity

I do not accept that phrase called 'down and out'
Describing one who knows what the game's about,
But, like the currency of our time,
Directs humanity deeper in the slime.
Those, who for one reason or another,
Have cut their apron strings with great grandmother
And maybe looking deep into the glass
They see what could perhaps have come to pass.
Men prefer to stand and drink 'pon the preciptic edge
Rather than engage monotony for a steady wage.

Admit that to see in us this is no sin
T'is only what you might have been,
For then you know just what you are,
Instead you rev that unpaid motor car.
There is no malice in the thought
This brief exchange thus far has brought.
Let mortgage men begin to learn
Their sales techniques that make you burn
Far more money than you earn,
Dear critic of the down and out.

Let's continue to examine your concern,
The charge is true that we
Who do not work should learn
To hold a place in the community.
I'll agree that we are dirty,
For we rise at four thirty
From sleep in cold openness.
But, ay there's the rub,
There's naught that won't scrub
To be clean is the path to Godliness.

So if visuals hurt with every glance
We should seek our dosser's image to enhance
In your eyes, maybe if that were true
You'd join us, not staying with work you do.
One thing that makes me sigh
With money when I buy
No one cares from who or whence it came,
So dirty money is accepted by clean men
And no one dies receiving it and then
Rich and prosperous they become.

Prosperous old man! What's your game
Trying to justify their unfortunate name?
What's my game? I'll now confess
It's nothing more and nothing less
Than unity. Let us cease deriding one another
And look upon our fellow man as brother,
Then providing that we seek to learn
Not to spend what we can't earn
We shall look together in the morning dawn
And a better deal provide for those unborn.

Part Two

Chapter Six

The Assault

Christmas came and went. The festive days were little different from ordinary ones for those with no roof over their heads. London streets were empty of the hustle and bustle, few shops were open, few pubs kept normal hours, and the majority of welfare and social units had closed. There was little to do for the vagrant. But the sun shone, and the ducks quacked. Jon, with enough money in his pocket for food and beer for two days, felt tranquil at that moment with where he was and why he was there. He quickly dismissed thoughts of his previous years with his family, thoughts of laughter, warmth, plenty of good and rich food, and wine in abundance. He sat in a park hut, propped up in a corner, with his feet on the bench and boots firmly on a plastic bag. With time and space around him he wrote in his pad.

```
Being alone did not come easily, but once loneliness,
like no man's land, was crossed I knew there was
no other way to live. When I shared convention's
facade living was easier. 'Outside' tested aloneness,
and in privation aloneness was like a protective leprosy.
I felt like the worm just managing to keep ahead
of the first plough. I saw in being alone a citadel
which would become worthwhile, without life as a forfeit
of course. It was not easy. Charades away the
character-punctured other life was like the one day
season of the May butterfly. The butterfly flew
by instinct, it knew not its destination.I felt like
the butterfly but for a different reason, the **need**
to follow the direction where instinct points. I
too did not know my destination. But I had this
sense of urgency, this need to communicate. Inside,
```

things were now stripped away and could at least be trusted. In aloneness, accusation was heightened in the senses like steel, proven in reality. Previously ignorance had damped awareness.

I was on my journey though in using 'the word' to convey I had to avoid the bric-a-brac of the past, comfortable cliches, compositing platitudes. I found I now had an earthy instinct that could be trusted. Hurt humanity had to be protected, not patronised. Words were killing more people than the wildest gunmen had ever killed. Pragmatism was no cure. Dogma was in the lethal race, and all that was left seemed to me to be on the betrayers' list. I could not think of surrender for anything less than humanity. Lip-service was necessary only to survive as I skirted cities of assassins permuting past mistakes. How to get through the mind-fields? In words every second one was a religious mind-field, and in the deed many were missionaries of logical madness. It was as though 'knowing' would soon be outlawed with God used as public enemy No. 1.

That's enough for today. Sitting huddled on that bench hasn't half made me stiff. Now I must foot it fast for a cuppa and a bite. Going to avoid charity as long as I can. Good show it was down at the Shelter over Christmas. Peeped in but didn't stay. Pity the charities can't extend their feeling of goodwill throughout the year. Bet the do-gooders get a lot of satisfaction themselves from what is known as 'making sacrifices to help the poor'. Bet they talk about it to their friends and get an ego trip. Wonder if that's why they do it? Keep my beer drinking till tonight. There must be one pub open in the whole of town. It's a damned awful place over public holidays. No wonder the suicide rate rises. Look at me, walking fast with no real place to go. Just filling in the endless hours.

Sunday came round quickly. Jon, rested for once after a good night's sleep in Rolling-stock hotel, felt in the mood to speak more aggressively from his stepladder in the Park.

He put his verbal confrontation with a police officer, who was frog marching a down-and-out to a van, well to the back of his mind. On arrival in the Park Jon saw that the crowd, taking advantage of the holiday break, seemed bigger than ever.

He collected the stepladder and stood patiently, waiting for the crowd's attention. Then he climbed the ladder and he said solemnly, "Big Brother is here." He waited for a moment to see the reaction. The stony faced silent men seemed to go tense. The crowd was still. So he continued.

"Humanity is being bound hand and foot, and we are all standing by watching from the touch line. We watch while pragmatists chip away at this country's many imperfections. This cannot be fought with tools of democratic naiveness. How much are each of us prepared to lose to defend the right to walk the streets in safety, to prevent more no-go areas arising?" He looked around for approval. "Is it worth a personal sacrifice to stop the aged from living in fear? It was these people who served our country with distinction in the last war, and it is on the backs of these people that most of us walk in our lives of material comfort. Why is fair play now being substituted by gamesmanship?"

The crowd had swelled into a mob and there was a murmuring undercurrent. It seemed as if malcontents, discontents and plain evil violators were jostling around, waiting for an opportunity to fracture the equanimity of the afternoon. They started to goad Jon. He shouted above the crowd, "Fear injections of the ilk that you people create are worse than disease. Disease can only kill us, but fear we are compelled to live with. Fear producing, like Arab or Jew baiting, is a crime against living whoever does it. There is only one race, our human race."

The noise was greater than ever. Angry voices insulted the realm admitting their involvement in the early growth of terrorist murder and riot, declaring vengeance was their aim and petrol bombs were the answer to the meek and mild dialogue of fools like Jon. The Special Branch with their mask-like faces stayed unmoved. There was a bus full of support police parked nearby, but they took no action.

Must have expected trouble this afternoon. Why all these extra police? Why this antagonistic mob? Hope something I have said has sunk in. Perhaps that's why they're angry.

Annoyed that the Special Branch were doing nothing to quieten the mob he called for silence so he could continue to talk. Miraculously the crowd responded.

"Now you have all heard that noise of dissent. You have all heard the abuse thrown at me and the boasting of evil and the airing of threats. Why is this not stopped? Why are the police silent? They are certainly here in abundance. They're the ones that don't move. Perhaps they are happier driving around in their white cars, blaring their horns reinforcing traffic regulations. That's much easier than being on the beat meeting the public and dealing with crime on the spot. Where is the policeman of previous years who was approachable and the citizen's friend? It's less hassle for them to fill their books with petty theft charges than to tackle serious crime." Jon watched the faces of the Special Branch either darken or redden. "Where is the authority in our land? Why is it that a crowd like you are publicly allowed to speak of arson and terrorism? Why are you all so proud of it? Where is there care for your homes or your families?" Feeling the anger in Jon's voice, the crowd were restless and began a swaying movement.

"Cool it, cool it," said a Special Branch man. The crowd took no notice.

Jon continued addressing the mob, "You have made this place a hunting ground for packs of organised political jackals who barrack everything from reason to patriotic fervour. The only speakers you leave alone are the religionists pontificating about the next life." Jon turned his comments away from the action of the crowd to matters of greater importance. He saw groups of tourists clicking their cameras gleefully to capture on film the coarse human safari unfolding before them. The door of the waiting bus had been opened and there was movement inside. Jon continued, "I have spoken about some of the weaknesses of authority. I have pointed out the miscreant ways of us all. Who is going to alter the coarse direction of contemporary power? How is the injustice which is splitting the realm apart going to be made into justice? How can some of the existing inhuman structures be demolished?" He spat out the staccato questions, one after another. "Around us all skullduggery works, often with official authority. There are too many philosophies to hide behind. Who is going to work for change? Are any of you? Or are you going to rest content dropping bombs on innocent people?"

As a section of the crowd broke into a roar the largest secret policeman stepped to the front, "I told you to cool it, and well you know it." The other policemen started to come out of the bus. "Had enough of you today, causing a breach of the peace you are." The crowd sensed trouble, they were well versed in the art of disappearing. Only the tourists were left looking bewildered. Jon left too, without a word to anyone.

They'll pick me up sooner or later. Am having too many brushes with the law for comfort. Pity I can't be more on their side. The thin blue line is basically a necessity for the country's social survival, but I seem to run into the negative side of their efforts.

He walked up Piccadily aiming for Covent Garden where he had found a small tea bar run by a family which was open night and day, seven days a week.

Jon was on the island in the middle of Whitcomb Street, he planned to go underground at Leicester Square, using the toilet facilities as he travelled. His mind was on the crowd, their agitation, their anger. Suddenly he felt a strong hand on his shoulder while he was waiting for the traffic to stop.

"You are under arrest," said a heavy man in civilian clothes. Without looking round, Jon flung off the man's grip, wove through the on-coming traffic and reached the pavement. But the heavy man moved faster and captured him on the other pavement and began to subject him to knuckle sandwich treatment, so heavily that Jon felt his assailant must have a problem. The assailant, having pinned Jon up against the wall, accused him of resisting arrest, and, for the first time, identified himself as a police officer.

"You shouldn't be surprised at my reactions. Anyone who has got any sense is going to resist. A surprise from behind without warning is bound to induce a defensive move," replied Jon and then added cheekily, "no wonder you've already got two black eyes."

His remark seemed to generate more fury, as the official thug, ignoring a gathering crowd, tried to batter Jon against the concrete wall, but although the official was a taller man, Jon was able to fend off any serious damage to himself. Soon a senior police officer appeared through the crowd, and ordered the thug to get into the police car.

Don't like the look of this much. It's my first physical brush with the law. Had plenty of verbal tiffs, but nothing so violent as this. My! It was a cool and callous way to get me hooked. How are other people able to cope? Not everyone knows how to defend themselves. That was one thing I did learn at the orphanage, and when a P.O.W., boxing and self-defence. Always thought it might stand me in good stead.

Jon took a quick look around. The crowd, eager spectators while the beating was going on, drifted away, not laying themselves open to be called upon as witnesses. Only one well-dressed man stepped towards the police officer.

"Whatever this man has done," he said, "You've no right to treat him like that. I shall report this incident to the nearest Police Station."

"Do that, but mind your own business now, or I'll arrest you too," replied the officer. That shut up the well dressed man who disappeared into the crowd, and Jon did not know if they would meet again. Very quickly a large square police van, well shuttered, arrived and six official heavies jumped out. Jon was viciously marched towards the van with his hands held behind his back by two of the heavies. On arrival at the Police Station he was charged with violent assault against an officer of the law. He was put into a large smelly cell.

Knew this would happen, sooner or later, 'cos of my public speaking and my tiffs with the police. Didn't expect the violence. Most upsetting. Much worse than I imagined. How do others cope who've never been in a cell before? At least I have known hardship in terrible conditions and know I can survive. For a first experience it must be terrifying, specially when the police are of the same nationality. I didn't somehow expect unprovoked violence from the British police. The Gestapo were different, anything from them came as no surprise. Blast you, can't you leave me in peace?

The observation slit in the cell door was opened frequently and shut with a loud bang. Slowly the seriousness of his situation dawned on him. The first arrival in Jon's cell was another Senior Police Officer.

"I'm Head of the Department dealing with terrorist activities," said the official, his large belly thrusting against the serge uniform.

"Me? A terrorist? Don't make me laugh," Jon was so surprised he tried to crack a joke. Then he went on a different tack. "I can see you are of a high status because you are more civilised in your approach. I know what has been said and because of that I've been put here, but don't waste your time trying to hook me up on some phoney charge, for if you know anything about me you will know

I am as much opposed to the violence of those terrorists as you are. In fact if you had been at some of my public speeches you might have been able to arrest some of those very same terrorists who you could have incriminated on their own statements as they tried to undermine me. Surely your underlings reported back to you?"

The Police Officer began to look embarrassed. Jon pressed on with his views. "I know you're too intelligent a fellow to jeopardise your own career by getting involved in whatever conspiracy is going on, for surely I sense there is a conspiracy."

"O.K., O.K., calm down a bit," soothed the Police Officer, "I must go and report. It won't be long before someone comes to see you." He left the cell, and Jon breathed a sigh of relief. "First scene over, and he wasn't heavy, thank goodness."

After several minutes another group of five arrived, four in uniform, and one civilian. The policeman with three stripes acted as spokesman. "This gentlemen is the Police Doctor." He pointed to the man in ordinary clothes. "It is understood you have made complaints about violence and that you have pains in you stomach. The Doctor is here to examine you on the grounds of this complaint."

Now I must think fast. What's the reason for this strange statement? I haven't complained about pains in my stomach. I must stop this bizarre state of affairs. If I let them check me, they will probably beat me up afterwards, why else the four men? I couldn't stand up to that, that I'm sure.

He addressed the Doctor. "Sir," he said, "I turn to you in your role of a Medical Practitioner, and in that role you must assess whether I tell the truth or not. I want to inform you that the statement made by the Sergeant is a lie. I have made no complaints about any pains in my stomach, and I wish to confirm that I have no internal injuries now, only facial bruising inflicted by the police. So if these thugs get ideas into their heads that they can beat me up after you have gone that is something you will have on your conscience."

The Sergeant cut in. "So you weren't beaten up?"

"I was," replied Jon, "but I have no pains." When the delegation left the cell he muttered out loud, "thank God for that. Perhaps I'll be left alone now!" Later that evening he was bailed out in his own cognisance, and ordered to appear at Court at 10.00 am the following morning. The Duty Officer handed him a piece of paper on which was written the address of the man who was prepared to witness in his defence. Jon trudged the streets wearily till dawn after his shift at the pub, upset and ill at ease. He breakfasted on tea and toast, and appeared at Court at the scheduled time. This Court appearance was a celebrated farce. Jon sought to go for trial where a jury could be involved, but the magistrate seemed unwilling to listen. The case was adjourned for a month, and Jon was told he was to put his request at his next appearance. There had been no chance for the vital witness to give his evidence. Jon met the man on the Court steps who told him that he had been to the Police Station the day before, and made a written statement on what he had seen of the thug's behaviour. Jon thanked him profusely, confirmed the date of the next trial, and the man promised he would be there. Jon was free for a month on bail.

Don't feel much like working at the Pub any more. Too many questions, and too much aggro. Must try something else. Funny that I should feel so low. Got a bad taste in my mouth. Must buck myself up before next Sunday, and more speaking. Got to keep up the momentum. I'll go and sit in St. James's. That's always soothing.

"'Ullo, Guv. Bit rough are yer? Oi watched all that were 'appening. 'Ad a bad time in the cell? Didn't rough yer up, did they? Got a month on bail, 'ave yer?" It was the thief, bright and perky and looking well monied.

Though angry at having his privacy invaded, Jon produced a smile. "Well, well, well, what is it that you don't know abut me? How do you manage to find it all out, so close to the Law, yet so much sought after by them."

"Oi've me ways," winked the thief. "And now Oi've been told it's time yer left London for a bit. Mustn't get into trouble when on bail. Can see yer'll speak again, given 'alf a chance. Mustn't speak again till yer've bin to court. Got a plan for yer, Oi 'ave. Come wiv me and meet Ben."

With nothing better to do Jon agreed. "Nothing to lose have I?" But don't expect me to agree with what Ben suggests, whoever Ben may be."

"Ben's O.K.," said the thief, "'E's got more money than 'e lets on. Too many irons in the fire. Does more fiddles in 'alf an 'our than Oi do in a week. Nice chap though. Yer be likin' 'im." Jon was very quiet as they walked down Beak Street, across Regent Street and into Conduit Street.

Looking at the street names Jon chipped, "if you go on much further you'll be in Mayfair. Don't tell me your Ben lives in Mayfair. Not the right kind of place for the likes of me. Nor for the likes of you for all I know." The thief made no reply. Goaded Jon continued, "how do you know everybody? How do you know about me? Take me to your leader." Still no reply. "I don't think you need to resort to crime, so why do you do it?"

At last the thief replied, "the more Oi get the more Oi 'ave to give away. That's what makes me life tick. Gets the old adrenalin flowing. Yer do yer work wiv words, Oi do my work by nicking. Now we're quits. 'Ere's Ben's 'ide out. Pretty good, ain't it?"

Jon looked at the shallow steps, and the large wood door with black knocker. Somebody from Ben's circle silently opened the door, and equally silently took Jon and the thief upstairs, wide curved stairs with a well polished curved banister. They came to double doors which opened equally silently.

"Hi there, Tucks, glad to see you." The thief moved across

the room and slapped a great man across the shoulders. He was the broadest man Jon had seen for a long time, and he had a large florid face and bright blue steely eyes, which seemed to unpick everything they looked at.

"Good to see yer, boss," replied the thief. "This is Jon. You know all about him."

"Hi there, Jon. Tucker has sent word about you."

I must remember that the thief's name is Tucker, at least that is what he says it is to this man, Ben. I bet he has a lot of other names as well. I'm going to play it cool till I can find out what this vast creature wants of me. Don't want to get indebted to him. What a strange set-up. No shortage of money here, that's for sure.

"Good morning," said Jon rather formally. "You seem to know more about me than I do myself. Tucker there said you had some plan for me. What's it all about?"

"Sit down, man, sit down. Have a brandy, or a beer? What about a smoke?" Ben effortlessly played the part of host.

"I'll have a brandy, thanks. No smoke." Jon sat on a black leather pouffe, very conscious of his shabby clothes.

Ben turned to Tucker. "You can go now, mate. Thanks for coming along. Be seeing you, usual time, usual place."

"Bye now, Guv," replied the thief. He turned to Jon. "Oi'll be watchin' for yer when yer come back. Got to take yer speakin' more easy." He walked out of the room moving silently as if he had been a thief all his life.

"Now, I'll tell you what it's all about," said Ben placing a large brandy on the small table by Jon's chair. Ben began, "I know you're a bit of a hot potato at the moment. I know why you are where you are, trying to instigate change. Must say, it's a bit of an uphill task, eh?" He laughed and his fat stomach, his jowls, and his lips wobbled like a stiff blancmange. Jon found Ben somewhat revolting. He waited silently. "It's like this. I'm trying to produce a film. It's short, has a small cast, and is set in the country by the sea. We have chosen North Devon for it, Saunton Sands actually. Do you know the place? I have allowed myself a month to do it. We want you to take a small part."

Jon burst out laughing at the proposition. "I'm such a bad actor. Why, I even had to be sacked when I was a stand-in for a statue. I kept on blinking, I was far too human. I'd be no good on the film set. Been acting in real life most of the time, and look where it's got me."

"You'll be got in even stranger places if THEY get you while you're on bail. Going to Devon will get you out of harm's way for the month. There are no strings attached. Once the month is over it's finished. You'll get board and lodging, and a small amount of money. Can't be much because we are doing it on a shoe-string. The film is going to be called 'The Cross and the Double Cross.' In its way it too is a radical protest. Come on man, take it. It will solve a lot of problems."

"But what about my public speaking?" asked Jon.

"Forget that for the moment," said his persuader. "Our main concern is to keep you out of trouble."

Who is this 'our' that he talks about? I don't think he wants anything more from me. I feel he has my welfare at heart. I don't like the man, but I'll be doing a job of work, so I'm not accepting something for nothing. If it wasn't me, it would be someone else. Give me a break. God, I need a break. Some of the poor buggers under Westminster Bridge have been there for years. They're so low they've forgotten what it is like to want a future. Mustn't let myself get like that. Got to keep on with my work and my speaking. Maybe some day someone will read what I've written.

"You're in a dream, Jon. What about an answer to my question?" Ben's voice brought Jon back to the present moment.

"O.K.," said Jon out loud. "I'll come. When do you want me to be ready?"

"Wednesday morning, here, 9 am. If you come earlier, you can have a bath and shave. Might be a good idea to get another jacket and shirt. Now, whatever you do, keep a low profile." Ben did not even bother to say goodbye, he turned to his desk and started to study some papers.

Suppose he's used to seeing lots of people. Now I'll give notice to that pub, and then tomorrow go back to my old friend Herbert in his so-called shop and try and re-kit myself. I wonder, do I smell that bad that it's necessary to offer me a bath? Can't smell myself, in fact can't smell much these days except bad air and fumes.

Jon spent the next two days very quietly, keeping well away from anyone in uniform. On Tuesday he lived on tea and an old piece of cake that Herbert in the tiny shop had offered him. Herbert had scrummaged around and found another jacket and a polo necked sweater and some old fashioned underpants. Jon laid all his money on the table, it was less than a pound, and Herbert accepted it without looking up. Several hours were spent just talking, it was as if the old man was starved for company. Jon told him part of the story of the last few days, and Herbert listened intently, nodding from time to time. Jon promised to call again, and when he said this the old man's face lit up. Jon was glad he had paid him a visit, welcomed his change of clothes, and once again walked out into the night.

The rendezvous on Wednesday passed without a hitch, and after a bath and a shave he felt equal to any of the gang who were to be with him. There were two car loads involved, and on the journey it was explained to Jon that there were four actors in the film, a policeman, an odd looking beggar in a wheel chair, a priest, and a young girl. There was also a curious time machine. He was to play the part of a priest. Again Jon burst out laughing.

"Me, a priest? With my red hair, beard, and suspect past?"

Although it was still January, the weather was warm, and the skies were blue. The film crew and actors spent most of the days on or near the beach. The script of the film had few words, and expressed the fantasy in the girl's mind. Jon proved his words were true, he was no actor. In spite of the support he received, as well as being dressed up in a priest's regalia, he stalled.

"No way can I lift up the knife and kill the beggar. Tomato Sauce and all. He looks at me with those big eyes, and I can't even pretend. You'll have to think of something."

The producer used his wits. He asked Jon to pull the knife from behind the beggar, looking angry as he did so. They then reversed the film. Jon enjoyed the time spent away from the filming. There was plenty to drink and eat, but he had difficulty in disguising his need for food. Ben had given him some money in advance, so Jon was able to stand drinks round for round. The sea air, the good food and the company made him feel really well. Unfortunately the month allowed for filming was not enough, so Jon had to leave before it was finished. This put everyone to much inconvenience, for all the scenes that Jon had acted had to be re-done. It appeared nobody minded the inconvenience, the crew and actors were occupied, paid, and in no hurry to return to London. Jon journeyed alone to London to continue with his conflict with the law.

CHAPTER SEVEN

Gaolbird

Jon appeared at court at the appropriate time. He could not see his witness anywhere. He hoped his case would be heard in the main Court where the press were allowed, but his hopes were shattered when he was ushered to the top of the building and to a smaller Court room where there was no press and still no sign of the witness. A solicitor and counsel did not appear until ten minutes before the start of the case: there was no time for Jon to explain his side of the story. He felt sure events were being manipulated to his disadvantage. He again asked for trial by jury, but his request was not heard. This time his bail was withdrawn and he was to be put in gaol so that a medical report on his state of mind could be assessed before sentence was passed. Another Court appearance was to be held in fifteen days. Jon fumed at the Magistrates and at the course of events, but he was quickly marched out of Court and driven back to a prison cell.

He took stock of his situation. He was in a single cell, but there were already two occupants in it. One had been charged with violence against the police, and the other for petty theft. Jon thought about his own situation.

Doesn't seem too rosy for me. I seem to be a victim of bent policemen, then bent Magistrates. Suppose I get a bent psychiatrist. I'd be like putty in their hands, and they could have me put out of the way for as long as they like. I've always said words and ideas are one of the most important weapons. That's probably why they've nicked me. My ideas are too dangerous. Better than the pack of lies that other people put out, and get away with. Now I must dip into my well of self-survival, and keep one ahead of them in my mind. Think I can withstand any physical violence. Difficult to know what to expect. Still, in a detached sort of way, it might be interesting.

After a short while a constable opened the cell door, and escorted Jon to a small room, obviously used for interviewing. Sitting at the desk was a young man, wearing a checked jacket and flamboyant tie.
"I'm the psychiatrist. They call me in when I'm needed. Now what's the problem."
"Well, you do surprise me," replied Jon. "I'm old enough to be your father, and here you are telling me I have a problem. It's your lot that have the problems."
"Seems odd, sir," said the young man and smiled a boyish smile. The boyish smile and the respect which the young man, though senior by reason of his medical status, offered to Jon made Jon breathe a sigh of relief and enabled him to feel he would put most of his cards on the table, and not play games with defensive talk. In fact the two hours they spent together became quite enjoyable.
Finally the psychiatrist stood up, "Well, sir, I've really enjoyed talking to you. I can assure you I will present a glowing report as to the state of your mental health. You've nothing to worry about on that score. In fact, I wish you well. But, in my official capacity, I must ask you to stay within the law."
With twinkling eyes he held out his hand. "Thanks a lot," said Jon. "There's good and bad come in all disguises, and you seem to be one of the good. I'm glad to have had a talk to you. As for staying within the law, I don't know. It's them that seem to invade my areas of privacy." They both laughed, and the psychiatrist left the room. Immediately the constable appeared and ushered Jon back into his cell.
He was again put in with two other men in a different

cell meant for a single prisoner. They were monosyllabic, and heavy people. Jon tried to find a common ground, but there was none. They were no trouble, just came and went, like zombies, at meal times and to the latrines. They did not snore or cough and spit.

One day after Jon had been to the washroom he came back to his cell to find it empty. The two other inmates had been removed to another wing. As he was putting his towel on the hook he looked at his locker. Something had altered. He looked inside, and saw some drugs which were not his amongst his possessions.

There's danger here, those zombies were put here for a purpose. By causing no friction THEY hoped to get me off my guard. Someone is trying to set me up. I'm going to make a bloody great fuss.

He banged on the door, first with his fists, then with his shoes. "Warder, Warder," he called. An angry warder came rattling along, his keys jangling.

"What the hell do you want?" he asked, "what's all this noise about?"

"What the hell do you expect me to do with these drugs that I've just found in my locker," came Jon's quick reply. "They're not mine, never used them. Must belong to the fellows who've just left. If it's your lot that's planted them I should like to know the reason why. I've met enough deviousness in my case without being made to look suspect for trafficking in that muck."

"I'll report the matter," was all the warder said, collecting the offending packets he left abruptly, locking up the cell again. Jon heard no more about the drugs.

Another trivial incident helped to make a small landmark to pass the fifteen day's incarceration. All the prisoners had to do small domestic duties. Jon was detailed to hand out the fruit for the day, one apple per prisoner.

"When that black bastard comes along," said a cross-eyed

warder with thick lips and a cauliflower ear, "give him a shrivelled little one. Can't bear them blacks. Cause us more trouble than anyone. Send them all back to where they came from, that's what I say."

"Then would you be prepared to do the kind of work they do? Would you like your son to be an underground porter, a hospital cleaner or road sweeper? That's why they're here. To help us do the jobs that no one else wants to do. Can't see you turning your hand to do that kind of work. You want a cushy number, don't you? You make me sick. Just because some of them get into trouble it doesn't mean that the lot are bad. It makes good media headlines to report bad news, and minority groups are easy to show up."

"Shut your trap," said the warder. "When I want your opinion I'll ask for it. I was told you were a cheeky bastard. Quite right too."

Jon began to give out the apples to the line of men. When he saw the coloured lad's turn coming up, Jon chose the biggest and juiciest apple, and with a flourish handed it to the fellow.

"Hey, that's fine," said the lad with a grin from ear to ear. "Best I've had for ages. Thanks a lot. It's made my day."

Whatever you've done, you've got the face of an angel. Can't imagine it was too serious. Must try and get a talk with the lad. He might be here 'cos he'd no one to defend him. Wonder what he does? Could be he's on his own with no family or friends? Could be he's caught up in the drug racket. Somehow don't think it's that.

Jon was not on his own for long in his cell. Another prisoner was led through the door. This man did not stop talking. What a difference from the other two silent occupants.

"Seen you in the Park," said the newcomer. "I've even

listened to you."

"Oh," said Jon. "It's a coincidence to find you in the same cell as me. Are you in for a rigged up charge or are you in the nick for true?"

"Rigged up charge? What do you mean, rigged up charge?" The newcomer sounded uneasy.

Ah. I've a sneaky feeling you're in here to find things out about me. Too eager to be an associate of mine. Came to mention the Park too quickly. Wonder what he wants to find out? Perhaps he thinks I'm under orders from some party or other who are using me to upset our so-called democratic way of politics.

"Tell me what you're in for," asked Jon, keeping his suspicions to himself.

"Loitering with intent, and that's all I'm going to say about it." The newcomer seemed quite put out. Jon listened as the man collected his wits, and started to talk, and as he talked he shot the most impertinent questions towards Jon.

"You must think I'm a nut-case," Jon said to the newcomer, weary of this camouflaged cross-examination. "Do you really think I don't see through what you are trying to do? The answers I have given you are all wrong, and you've wasted your breath. I know full well you are a plant trying to find something that your so-called masters think I should tell them. But you tell them from me, that my ideas are my own, that my ideas and thoughts are being passed around, and that ideas are the most powerful weapon anyone can have. **They** know ideas are dangerous. No matter what they do to me, apart from killing me, or imprisoning me for ever, they cannot stop my ideas from growing. Tell your masters that I work for no one. I have found no one yet whom I can trust. And I certainly don't trust the likes of you, in spite of all your grand talk and name dropping." Both men were glad when the warder came again, and under the pretext of an interview with a Senior Official the newcomer was led out of the cell. "Good riddance," Jon called out, "and now for some peace." Jon lay on the bed and tried to read one of the books from the library.

He ate the food with relish, most of the other inmates looked glumly at the helpings on their plates. "This is a feast when you've had an empty stomach for some time," he said.

"You look O.K.," replied a young lad. "Don't look starving to me."

"Some days are not as easy as others," Jon replied and left it at that.

Soon it was time for the next Court appearance. Although Jon had been promised the services of a Defence Council, none appeared. It was not until he was in the cells at the Court waiting for his turn in the dock did two gentlemen appear.

"Good-day gentlemen," said Jon with a sarcastic voice. "And may I ask whom I have the pleasure to meet at this late hour? I'm told I'm the last case to be heard this morning, so fortunately there is a little time to spare."

"I'm your solicitor, and this gentleman is the Defence Counsel."

"It's like putting a quart into a pint bottle," retorted Jon edgily. "There's so much background information for me to give you in order that I have a fair trial that it would take ten hours rather than two. I feel that you've been sent at this late hour just to put things on a legal footing, and for justice to appear to be done. I can only tell you the ribs of the case." He had just started to make his statements when the original thug appeared at the door, the thug who had molested him on the traffic island, and then beaten him up.

"And now look who's here. Sleeping Beauty just woken up."

"Yer next on the list. Not last as was written down. Now 'op it quick," the thug spoke in a thick voice.

Jon turned to his counsel. "This is just a bit of tactical undermining. Been like this from start to finish. They've got the power, the prestige, and can call any tune they like. I'm the underdog without the financial means to fight back. You watch what happens in Court. I'll scarcely get a word in edgeways. They'll find me guilty. Willing to bet on it?"

The Counsel scowled. The solicitor said in a mincing voice, "You are making matters worse, talking like that."

Throughout his varied experiences, Jon had been under various secret police set-ups much more lethal than this present occasion, and he rode it like an operatic tea party. He offered no opposition, the Counsel was as good as a sick headache and the solicitor even worse. As Jon knew what the outcome would be he made no visible sign when the verdict was announced. He was to pay a stiff fine for assault on the policeman, and was bound over to be of good behaviour for the next two years.

There goes most of my paltry savings. Bet they knew I'd got something stuck away for emergencies. But how did they find out? What's in the account is the same amount as the fine. S'pose all my private affairs are swopped around on various authorities' computers. Don't like that idea very much. S'pose I'd got VD. Wouldn't want people to know that, but how could I stop it, once I'd had medical attention? Doesn't say much for the twentieth century if the individual has no privacy left.

Aloud he said to the warder who was escorting him out of the Court. "Guess I'll be rooked for the services of the two legal blokes, useless as they were. That's what makes me angry. Money given for useless services, everybody being on the same side, and me alone on the other side. All things considered our legal system is probably the most liberal of all the countries in the world. Yet they do bad things, like today's farce, and manage to make it look as if justice was being done. However devious the acts of authorities they all hide behind a profile that talks of liberty of the individual. Liberty, my foot, unless the individual has deep pockets. But even so, we're luckier here than in other places."

"Best you just keep these ideas to yourself, sir," said the warder. "You'll only get into more trouble. Do what you want to do, but keep out of trouble. I've been here long enough to know what it's like always coming back here, time after time. Gets them down at the end. Wouldn't like to see you got down, sir. You just take care."

"Well, well, I really think you mean what you say. That sure is a treat." He turned and shook the warder by the hand, and walked abruptly out of the Court. He did not want to meet his legal advisers again. Back on the streets Jon was momentarily confused. He walked slowly away from the Court building, aiming for St. James's Park.

Oh, for the fresh air and colours of the Park! Always does me good. Afraid that's a foretaste of what is coming to me, I'm sure it is. If I'm going to stay on this course, driven by my daemon, to oppose injustice I must expect much heavier treatment. But I really must try to do what I must do without crossing swords with the police. It's eerie how they've found out I've had that small amount in the bank. It's eerie the way they can find out all about a person nowadays, and from computer to computer pass around to lots of people everything they know. Another incident of invasion of privacy. Sometimes I feel I'd rather like to go back to horse and carriage travel, then news wouldn't travel so fast. I'm going to hang on to my money for a while, and not pay the fine. Wonder what will happen? Must find work fast. Got to eat to live.

After trying well over thirty places, mostly in the pubs, or small restaurants with no success Jon started to feel worried.

Must look more untidy and more tramplike than I feel. I'm still the same inside. Coat's a bit shabby, and boots are dirty. Haven't any socks, but people can't see that I haven't any underwear. Wonder what's putting them off? Must have a jolly good bath and clean up a bit. The cells weren't really dirty, but the whole place makes me feel I need to wash the experience away. Why am I fussing? I went three months in Poland without taking off what few clothes I was allowed. No wonder the bugs enjoyed me. They ate more out of me at night than I had to eat all day.

The next morning after a cold night huddled in an alley way off Mortimer Street, his legs and feet in a black plastic bag, he spent one of his precious shillings on a full bath with all the extras. He shaved, cut his hair and nails, washed his shirt and trousers, wearing his second very old ones while they dried. He tried to clean his shoes with wet toilet paper. The attendant looked on and then protested. "Come off it," he called. "This isn't a bleeding private 'ouse. Yer 'aving more than a bobs worth."

"Can't get work looking as I did," replied Jon. "I'll clear up after myself. Jolly good bath that. I could hardly get messages to my legs they were so stiff, and the hot water was just what I needed. What do you know about the large block of flats in Knightsbridge, backing onto the Park? They're advertising for a janitor. Thought I might have a try."

"Try that," said the attendant, looking more friendly. "Full up with aristocrats, ambassadors and big wigs in trade. Yer might get tips there." He gave Jon a look over. "Now that's be'er. Good luck to yer, and come again. I'll shut me eyes to yer washin' and cleanin'."

"I'll keep you to that," replied Jon. "If I get the job, we'll have a beer. I'd like to know about the grass roots of this area. It's not the kind of work I'd choose, but I've got to keep old man hunger away." Jon tidied his belongings into his holdall and with a cheerful grin left the attendant to his work. Slowly he walked away from the Fulham Road and up Sloane Street.

Used to feel at home hereabouts. I'm just an intruder now. But it's in these big houses, the restaurants and hotels that work is more available. Work I must have, so here goes. It's those poor suckers who have had the will to work squeezed out of them by their hopeless state that have to be pitied. Just because they haven't a home address they're condemned to a life of degradation. Living quarters offered by the Councils wouldn't be given to a lot of dogs, and the accommodation given by the religious are swamped with holy teachings. No one feels like being preached to when he's starving and cold. Can't the wretches leave the dosser with his self-respect? Damn the blasted Governments! Maybe one day the religious do-gooders might offer their help without the element of bribery, you have my cup of tea and you must believe in my God.

Jon brought himself back to his present predicament and steeled himself to meet the Manager of the flats. When he realised that much of his work was to be connected with the security of the property, he started a spiel about his period in Intelligence at the end of the war, giving the Manager the impression that he knew all about the devious ways of those who wanted to penetrate a concern such as the one he was being expected to look after. His newly scrubbed appearance must have impressed the Manager or there may have been no other applicants, but Jon was offered the job, his hours were to be from 2 pm till 10 pm. There was no food offered in the contract, but there was an electric kettle in the cubby hole in the basement where he was expected to sit when not busy. Jon accepted the contract, given a beige overall, and told to start on the Monday shift. He left the building in a sombre mood, not lightened by only having a few pennies in his pocket. He walked to Kensington Underground and with a wink and a nod he passed the ticket collector. He found the Circle line, and a seat in the corner of the front carriage and settled down to a sitting up sleep. He hunched himself low into his collar, and firmly grasped his holdall with his work and few possessions under his arm by the window. Sleep came quickly as if for making up for lost time. He woke refreshed to find himself crushed by people standing all around and he realised it was the rush hour. He surfaced at the next stop which he saw was Euston, and decided to spend some of his pennies on a cup of tea. He put his pad on the table and started to write.

```
Am I moving fast enough towards the purpose of my
journey?  Are there moments when it is better to
do nothing, than to do something for the wrong reasons?
Time hangs heavily with nowhere as a base.  I must
keep up my morale.  However many steps there are
in front is not of the greatest consequence once
I accept I cannot get back into the womb, I just
have to accept pleasure or pain, or both.  Then
I must go forward all the time, conscious of my
weaknesses, strengths and the destiny of humanity.
This insecurity is bearable where truth and love are
observed and further multiplied by entering into
sacrifice.  Like all life on this planet, Supreme
Intelligence can and will not hurt the concept of
life's dimension. No purpose or vigilantes can obstruct
life's absolute Intelligence.  How thankful I am that
I can still think thoughts on this plane, I feared
that hardship would dampen the flow.  I know that
servitude is the mind bender's backlash.
```

Bringing himself back to reality he made the effort to go back on the street and start walking again. He walked slowly along the back streets until he came to the City, and then delved underground again at the Bank and caught the train southwards. He immediately fell fast asleep, tucked well into a corner. But he was metaphorically caught with his pants down. He was woken up roughly by a shake on the shoulder. The train had drawn in at the terminal, Morden, and the cleaners were on the night shift.

"Wake up, wake up, man. You've overshot the mark. Where did you want to get to? No buses now, and no taxis either. Not that would bother the likes of you." Jon let that remark pass by, he was still bemused from sleeping.

"Sorry, chum, I'll be off. Thanks for waking me." Jon answered no questions. He walked to the station exit. It was a very dark cloudless night, and the stars were bright. He breathed the clean crisp air and felt refreshed, the air made him hungry.

Will fiddle with these chocolate machines. Never know your luck. Someone may have left something in it by mistake. Nothing in that one, or that. Now this one. Damn it, must have got jammed. Try again. Wow, my good luck's in. A whole bar of fruit and nut. Worth more to me than a million pounds at the moment. Won't last me long... It's such a glorious night... Might just as well be walking as sleeping.... Good to be alive.... Got a long way to go though, should imagine it's all of twenty miles. I'll try to get a hitch, but who'll want to pick up the likes of me?

He tried to hitch some of the sparse traffic going northwards, and turned away from a taxi who was stalking the curb looking for a fare. The taxi drew up alongside, and in the darkness of the night all Jon could see were two white slits of eyes, for the driver, a man from Barbados, was deep black himself.

Cheekily Jon called out, "Glad you've got your eyes open or I wouldn't have seen you. If it's money you're after I've got none."

The driver's attitude was a reproval on the remark about his colour, and Jon wished he had not said it. The driver said, "Jump in, mate." 'Jump in' meant to sit on a small box in the front free part next to the driver, usually kept for luggage. The flag was left up as the driver pottered towards the city.

After moments of sparring chit-chat Jon said, "How nice

to meet a refugee as far away from home as myself. You've got colour linked with dignity. Sorry for my stupid remarks."

"You get used to handling things like that," replied the driver. "Anyhow being black at night doesn't matter anyway. What does hurt though is when your daughter comes back from school and tells you that her teacher has told her that she has written down her nationality wrong. Even though she was born here in London, that bitch of a teacher told her she was not British. That's the kind of thing that hurts."

"Did it upset your daughter?"

"Sure it did. But she won in the end. She refused to rub out the word British, and the teacher had to settle for it. It's still odd, but after six years at that school, some families won't ask her back to their houses. There's nothing different about her except her colour, she speaks the same, she doesn't have any religious hang-ups, she dresses the same. Perhaps it's because I'm a taxi driver. Better that than being unemployed like some of the parents. Poor devils."

"How long have you been here?" asked Jon.

"Twenty years. Arrived when lots of us came to do low paid jobs. Started off at the stations, saved my money, and then bought a taxi. Been careful with my wages, and now I've got all I want, a lovely wife and family and work. I've caused no trouble. There's lots like us, we're no trouble. I was the first black man to have a taxi in London."

"That must have taken a bit of doing," said Jon.

"It did, believe me," replied the driver. "At the time it was considered a unique achievement, and **they** tried to do a documentary on me. Don't know who started the idea. Didn't want to involve my family, and thought they might use it for propaganda purposes, so I didn't accept. Would have helped from the money side, of course, they offered me a whack. Glad I refused though." They talked freely for the rest of the journey and soon they arrived at Shaftesbury Avenue.

"This is fine for me," said Jon. "I'm really grateful to you. You've probably guessed I'm a transplant like yourself, but unlike you I've left behind my own home and family. It's people like you who give me assurance that life is still worth pursuing. It's been really good to meet you, and thanks again for the lift. But that's a practical matter, not as important as the other intuitional one, but welcome all the same. Look there's a gang of youngsters coming. Bit drunk, I think. But they might give you a fare. Bye now."

The friendly man tooted on his horn and drove straight towards the animated group. Jon was delighted to think that the driver would get another fare for he was sure that Shaftesbury Avenue was well out of his usual beat at this time of night. He aimed for the tea counter in Covent Garden and spent the rest of the night chatting amongst the marketeers. One stood him an outsize mug of tea. It was very welcome. The next two days were very long, and Jon became hungrier and hungrier. His stomach seemed tied in knots, each knot rubbing painfully against the stomach walls.

I'll not spend my savings, and I'll not go for Assistance even though I could give Trevor's address. Perhaps this janitor job will give me a leg up. I must see if I can cope with life as it comes on my own. Got a good kip last night by that ventilator at Oxford Circus, so it's not all bad. God, I'm famished. I'll go and raid the rubbish bins in the Park. P'raps the picnickers have left something edible and clean. 'Xpect the pigeons or squirrels will get there first. Maybe life'll deal me out good cards again, like with the chocolate.

With this thought in mind he wandered through both Hyde Park and St. James's Park and found several packets still wrapped in plastic which the wild life had been unable to penetrate, ends of crisps, crusts, meat pies. He did not touch the pies fearing that the meat would be off. He also found a whole apple and some chewing gum. He settled down by the lake in St. James's to eat and to watch the birds. The weak March sun tried to warm him, Jon turned towards it and was thankful for all that was beautiful, and that he was still able to acknowledge the beauty all around him.

Chapter Eight

Knightsbridge

Jon reported to the Manager at the flats at 1.40 on the Monday as arranged. He looked reasonably tidy, having found a shirt with collar and tie which he bought on tick, explaining that he would take the money back the next Saturday. The Manager guided him carefully round the large block, showing him all the exits that had to be checked twice daily, at the beginning and end of his shift. He was to be responsible for the whole building, a building which was divided into twenty large and gracious flats for the well-to-do. He was shown the various alarms.

"This is just the sort of place for terrorism," explained the Manager, "we've got foreign ambassadors, and professionals. Most could be targeted. Your job's cleaning too, everywhere public, and deal with the rubbish. Should be fairly straight forward. But don't forget, clients are always right. That's sometimes quite hard," and he gave Jon a small smile.

As the need for ready money was of paramount importance, Jon asked for a day's wages in advance. Surprised for the moment, the Manager thought quickly and then agreed. He actually gave Jon the money for the day there and then, his cold demeanour relaxing.

"I'll have left the office before you knock off" said the Manager. "If you get into trouble here's the phone number of the Agents, but only phone if there is an emergency. Otherwise you're on your own. Now, I'll be off. I think I've shown you everything." The Manager left quickly.

You're in such a hurry I expect you've got a bit of skirt

waiting round the corner. Quite human underneath that coldness, actually got a smile from him. Doesn't seem too concerned about the place... Now let's take stock. One day's pay for one week. That's going to be tough. Should manage one meal a day. Can wash in the sink, that will save the bath money. Have to go short on the beer. Will have a talk with the landlord, and see if he minds if I hang around with only half a pint. Wouldn't be for more than an hour. Let's see what's in the cupboard. Good, there's coffee and sugar. I'm well away. Can always fill it up next week. Now I must off on my rounds. Any bugger of a thief could break in here. Could do it myself! There's no stopping anyone from coming up the fire escapes at the back. How can I know that the residents have locked their kitchen doors? From the look of these soft carpets there must be lots of money around. Wish I could kip down just on the carpet! Softer than many a place I've had these last months.

Dressed in his new brown overall, Jon was bending down picking up some leaves fallen from a flower arrangement in the corner of the front hall. He heard an autocratic voice calling to him. "Now, whose newspaper is that by the door? Newspapers shouldn't be left lying on the floor, my man."

Jon turned to see an elderly woman with blue rinsed hair, well wrapped up in a fur coat. From her accent he could tell that she was not British, but her manner aped that of the aristocracy. He replied slowly, "the paper is certainly not mine, ma'am, but I will of course remove it."

The furcoat seemed to glide past him. "Will you call the lift, please?" Jon pressed various buttons hopefully, he had not got his glasses on and hoped the lift would not end up in the cellar. With her nose slightly tilted away she waited for what seemed minutes, grinding her teeth, and when the lift arrived embarked on the journey to her flat without even an acknowledgement.

Jon performed his duties meticulously and when his wages

were delivered on the first Friday he felt like a millionaire, a weeks wages minus the day he had already been paid seemed a lot of money. That evening he left at 10 pm sharp, and went to the Cock and Sparrow where he was becoming a well known feature. People waited for him to pop in, then cornered him for a question and answer session. The landlord seemed glad to have him there. Jon tried to stand a round of drinks to all the people who had been generous to him during the week. When time was up he left the pub and walked out into the night.

Good crowd in that pub. Lifts my morale. Sometimes I feel there's more rapport soul to soul during a spontaneous talk than with all the trappings of familiarity. Who says it breeds contempt?

Still I've chosen to go it alone, and I'm content at that. I can do without the hostility of my well-meaning acquaintances, the police, the do-gooders and the Bible thumpers with their 'authority of the deity'.

I've got to find out in silence and contemplation whether there is anyone to report to, a kind of Supreme Intelligence. That's going to take strength, strength to reach for the principle of awareness and pass it on when I speak. Not so easy when the mind's disorientated by hunger and lack of sleep.

There's not much left in my pocket! Still it's better than last week, and I've survived that. Now to concentrate on my speaking in the Park. Mustn't let it get around that I work in those flats. **They** *could make it very difficult for me if they found out. It's a right crazy place there. Anyone could come in the back way. I'm glad I lock the front doors and they all have to ring to be let in. One old geyser fair took the pants off me, he did, because I kept him waiting a few minutes. They're so cocooned in their little shells they've no idea what life is all about. Now,* *what chances of a kip in Hyde Park tonight? Shrubs look healthy round Peter Pan. No one around? Good. Now the bedding down ceremony. Don't have to use the bushes for a pee. Just went in the pub. Plastic bags, here they are. One for each foot and one for my bottom. Quite comfy tonight, that's fine. What a ridiculous situation. Here am I, sleeping rough, and rather hungry. In the day I work in exclusive flats, guarding the so-called elite. Bet they've no idea that I either sleep under the stars, often in Cardboard Hall, or like the flotsam and jetsam use Rolling Stock hotel for the warmth. 'Xpect I'd be given the sack if they found out. Must keep myself tidy. Don't want to lose this job, could suit me well. Can write in the cubby hole, get my speeches ready for Sundays and I can keep warm for part of the day. Whatever happens, I am not going to take any tips, not like a servant. As long as they leave me my dignity I'll try and stick it. Must watch out for blue-rinse in the furcoat. She looks as if she could mean trouble.*

With his shoulders hunched, and collar and scarf around his ears, sleep soon blotted out any more thought, and he only woke to the noise of the litter cart being trundled around. He let it pass, then unwound himself. Stiff and cold, with piercing pains in his legs, he took a little while before he could stand on his feet. Morale rose when he jingled his few coins in his pocket as he walked towards the lakeside restaurant where he ordered tea and toast.

The first month working at the flats passed quickly. The Sunday sessions in the Park were drawing more and more people; when he arrived they drifted away from the other speakers to listen to him. The sessions tired and exhilarated him, and he was thankful to feel a sense of purpose. One mid-week afternoon, just after he had started his spell of duty and was on his round he saw blue rinse fumbling in her bag outside her flat. She looked really agitated.

"Can I help you, ma'am?" asked Jon.

"I can't get into my flat. I've tried one lot of keys, and

now I'm looking for another set. I think it's locked from the inside." She continued to fumble. "I've no more keys to try. What shall I do?" Her face crumpled, and she was no longer the arrogant woman of the newspaper incident.

"Should there be anyone inside the flat?" asked Jon.

"My husband. He's the Spanish Ambassador, and he's got a meeting later this afternoon. He was to have had a rest and a light lunch before his engagement."

Got to do a bit of quick thinking. Ambassadors are two a penny on the hit list these days. Just supposing someone has locked the door and is threatening him. Can see the back door open through the letter box. The old girl is in such a state, but I must try to do something. I'll have another go at turning the key, they get jammed sometimes.

He smiled reassuredly at blue rinse, and gave the door a mighty push with his shoulder turning the key as he did so. The door flashed open. The flat was empty, but with the back door open the curtains were flapping. Jon searched the flat and there was no sign of the Ambassador or any intruder.

"Ma'am, do you remember locking the back door? See, it's open? And are you sure the Ambassador said he would be in?"

"No, I don't remember about the door," she said all of a fluster.

"Where could the Ambassador be? Has he a club?" Jon didn't like to ask if he went to a pub.

"Oh yes, yes," said blue rinse. "I'll phone the Club." Smiles wreathed her face when she heard her husband's voice. "Well, that's that. Perhaps I'm a little forgetful. No?" She tried to be cocquettish. Jon felt the stirrings of angry feelings. Blue rinse then fumbled in her bag as Jon was about to leave. Remembering her disdainful performance with the newspaper, he felt disgusted that she thought she could buy him off with the two pounds that she offered him.

Supposing there had been a burglar, and the burglar had been armed. What would it have cost her then? Jon refused the money as tactfully as he could.

"Will you feel safe if I leave you now?" he asked.

"Yes, I will feel safe," she answered, and more graciously than before she asked, "why won't you accept the money?"

"Because, ma'am, if I accepted it you'd be robbing me of something. It's a privilege to be able to help a lady for nothing. There are very few things that are left to us, like chivalry for instance."

He turned and quietly left her to her own devices. The only other incident that made a landmark in the dull cycle of his duties concerned a swarthy gentleman. Jon listened in the lift to this gentleman conversing with his fellow country man who was a temporary tenant of one of the flats. Jon assessed they were both from North Africa, presumably Libya. The visitor had asked Jon for his help to carry some packages to an awaiting car, and although it was nearly knocking off time Jon felt it was his duty to offer his services.

I'm sure this is a lot of drugs. Feels just the right weight, all spongy and heavy. It makes me sick. Why all this night time movement? Why should I be involved in helping these crooks to undermine the morale of the country? We've had enough terrorism from you lot, and now this. Drug dealing. Wish I'd the guts to quit. Tell them I won't carry the stuff. But the job suits me fine to keep me going in the Park so I don't want to quit. But I feel really dirty inside. Why is it always decisions, decisions, decisions?"

When the two men handed a large note for Jon to accept, he refused saying angrily, "I know what is in those packages. You should be turned in for the Law to deal with you. Why should you get me involved?"

The two men looked bemused, then the visitor collected his wits. "You take damn care what you say and what you think," the older man said in a guttural accent.

"If I see it happening again, I'm off, and I'll be reporting it to the police. I'm not prepared to break the law. I'll not compromise again. You'd better watch it. Likes of you aren't welcome in this country." The elder man shook his fist. Jon turned on his heel and left them.

After this encounter Jon went straight to the usual pub, and drank his pint quickly. He was flustered and annoyed that he had allowed practical wants to override his principles. It was pay day and he had money in his pocket. He felt the need to unwind. He started to talk to those around him and once again had a captive audience.

"What **are** you?" asked someone. "Are you an actor? A writer? You keep us all so amused with your stories."

"A writer?" echoed Jon. "No one in their right senses could serve up that hypothesis. I'm illiterate in two languages. You only put 'X' to your name when you vote. 'X' is my name, even when I write a cheque."

"Cash only, from you," joked the landlord.

"Alright, I'll explain," said Jon getting into his stride, "I come from a long line of headless jesters who either told the right joke at the wrong time or the wrong joke at the right time, but whatever the combination, they failed to keep their heads. With this very good beer, I find it hard to keep mine, so drink up, and have a bumper toast with an illiterate jester who doesn't want any drink back in return. Give them all a drink, Governor," said Jon with mock lordliness.

"Not till I've seen the colour of your money, sir," said the landlord without offence. Jon slammed down a note from his wages, as if he had no care in the world.

"And for your courtesy as mine host in a world of beer slingers, have a drink yourself."

"Thanks, mate. It must be your birthday," said one of the listeners.

"Birthdays only come once a year," replied Jon. "My good fortune is an everyday event."

"Then you must have won the pools," said the landlord,

as he finished the round of drinks ordered by Jon.

"Not exactly. But I'm one of the few to make a success of failure." Jon realised that he was holding the attention of his small audience. "You see, gentlemen, there are so few of us who dare to admit failure." The bar went silent. Jon proceeded, his confidence primed with the beer on an empty stomach. "Now I failed at everything I ever did, from the innocent ability of early childhood when failing to be able to spell the most basic four letter words, right up to this glorious summer, and you know how hot it has been. Recently, while sauntering for about a half mile in the Park and raising my hat to my creditors I had to be treated for sun-stroke." There was a ripple of laughter and a clink of beer mugs. "You see, gentlemen, I will tell you something I'm sure you won't believe. I am a unique millionaire. I actually owe a million. My secretary works full time satisfying my creditors on one point alone, my health. For as long as I live they know they've got a chance of getting their money back."

"Not as long as you continue to play the role of big spender," chipped the landlord pleasantly. "But as long as you pay in cash, why should I worry?"

"There now," said Jon in mock despair. "Here is another example of failure. I have failed to convince our genial landlord that I'm credit worthy."

"But what do you really do?" persevered the same man.

"Like you, sir. I dramatize work for others."

"You asked for that," said the landlord chuckling. Jon excused himself and went outside to the toilets. On his return he found more beer lined up for him. He was no longer the focus of attention, and for this he was grateful. He put the liquid gun to his head, and listened to the conversation going on around him. The theatres and cinemas nearby had finished their evening performances and the pub was filling up. Sitting on his bar stool he found himself sandwiched between a talkative mercenary soldier and a formal elderly man who had the authority of a high powered executive. The mercenary related his experiences in a loud voice and made it appear that he was the only medal winner in each incident. Jon was silent, and the mercenary continued, "You know, I failed at Sandhurst. Didn't make the grade with the military. My father was furious, he's been a soldier all his life, and fought in the last war. He was right disgusted when I became a mercenary, in spite of all my successes. He's a stupid old buffer. I just hold respect for him, but that's all."

This remark angered Jon who interrupted and said, "if you had respected your father more you might have come to love him. After all, he was a patriot and did fight in the last war. **You** are nothing more than a mercenary."

"I am also a patriot," countered the mercenary, "for the country I choose to serve. I have their nationality as well as their medals."

Jon was getting angrier, the extra beer fuelling his feelings. "You must have murdered quite a lot of people to get those medals," he said provocatively.

"Watch it," said the mercenary. "You are insulting the honour of the unit I served."

"If we ever inhabit caves again," said Jon recklessly, "it will be because of men like you. A patriot I can understand, but a mercenary, never."

"I told you to watch it," said the mercenary, a big man and half Jon's age. He raised his fist threateningly.

"I won't punch you back," said Jon. Before Jon could duck away from his stool he found himself at the heavy end of the mercenary's fist. This opened up an old wound in his nose which splattered his face with blood. Three more blows followed which Jon parried with his raised arm. With all the experience of his younger days on the boxing booth when he took on all comers he knew that the great bulk of a man delivering the blows couldn't box. Fortunately the landlord intervened.

"You come on outside, I've not finished with you yet," shouted the angry mercenary now out of control.

"I've no intention of coming. You couldn't burst a paper bag. I'd floor you easily. Where is your self-respect? You hit a seated man twice your age and subdue the truth."

A customer who disliked the look of blood asked Jon to wipe his face. "You can see it, you do it," replied Jon brusquely.

"You'd better go, we're not used to having trouble in this pub," said one of Jon's fellow drinkers.

"The landlord hasn't asked me to leave, and I've no intention of going. In fact, with the landlord's permission, I'll have another pint." Silently, and so in sympathy, the landlord drew Jon another pint, turning away quickly taking no payment. Jon was given a damp cloth for his face, and the incident which had risen quickly ended. The tension was over, and Jon indicated to the landlord to fill the mercenary's glass. The truce was accepted.

As quiteness was regained in the pub, so quietness seemed to fill the night air. When Jon left the pub he felt the sharp winter tang was replaced by softer cool air, not bone seeking. The soil became damp and smelt of growing life, and when Jon dug his toe into the earth the insects scuttled, busy with new urgencies. Jon found a corner in the churchyard in Hyde Park Crescent, and watched the dark sky dawning around the chimney pots of the tall buildings. He was not aware that he had slept deeply, but as he felt so refreshed and exhilarated in the early hours he presumed he must have had enough to satisfy his needs. He was in no hurry to get his first cup of tea, there was no unfreezing of limbs to do, so he made sure he was out of sight and wrote in his pad.

```
It is a beautiful day today.  I slept on the right
side of the turf in the graveyard of an old London
church,  and then walked with my bare feet on the
good earth, as I did as a child, with only shillings
in my pocket.  I do not need more.  You are rich
with  only  a  few  bob,  and  poor with  a  fortune.
```

'Being' is enough, not 'to be' is not the question. Let real estate seek to shut out the sky for profit so that, in order to start their days, the whole world becomes slaves to expensive watches. If that futile song ever becomes true, let Britannia rule just one wave. May she never waive the rules. I shall never become a slave to protocol, convention and mindless lip service. Nor in the face of that one journey which we all take and where the destination is in doubt, will I shrink from new experience or take for granted the common place.

The innocent are swayed by verbal pressures and descriptions of standards and etiquettes that are supposed to be essential. Those who have regard for social progress are caught and declared a fugitive in their own environment to the detriment of untold well being by lesser intelligences. By mounting too many judgements on lies, our nation has suffered greatly. Techniques must be found to sustain the defensible and at the same time change yesterday's vulnerability. Can it be that now nobody cares? Is the lie factor not considered important enough to alter? Again I come back to the need for change. There was a time when a man's word was his bond, now the word is man's bond only when it pays to be.

But enough is enough. Thinking can be a crime against oneself, but to put some thought into print makes a forger look honest. The bank of human understanding, once lost, is hard to regain.

CHAPTER NINE

Dismissal and Dosser Arthur

Spring brought a fraction of ease to many in the twilight world. Tired and bedraggled scraps of humanity seemed to grow and stretch out, offering their cramped limbs to the warmth of the sun. The parks and benches along the Embankment were there for those who just wished to relax. One anxiety had been removed, the fear of the intense cold and the need to find the will power to combat the paralysing discomfort. Sleep came easily in the warm freshness, it was very different to the foul air breathed in the Undergrounds or in Rolling Stock Hotel. Jon knew that in many of the hostels open to vagrants the beds were so close together that the air was equally foul, heavy with the smell of dirty feet, unwashed bodies, urine and bad breath.

Glad I've kept away from the hostels. But remember, old cock, I've had two breaks when I've had no need to look for a roof, once in the cells, and once down in Devon. Twice I was fed and warmed. That helped to set me up. But it's been a bloody long winter, but not as long as for those other poor buggers. It's worse for them, most seem to have lost the will to want to work. Just living to survive or surviving to live, what hope can they hold? Specially when they withdraw from human contact... God, I'm fortunate... Just being alive is enough for me, there's so much I need to do. It's better with grub now and again, but the freedoms I have! Wouldn't give them up for a million pounds. Many people around the world, in concentration camps or gaols or whatever, would jump at the chance to be in my boots, defending the inarticulate. I'm making no great sacrifice, that's for sure.

He pushed open the door of the block of flats and went to his cubby hole. There was a note on the table saying that the Manager would be calling that afternoon to speak to him.

Can't think I've done anything wrong. The only fly in the ointment is blue rinse. I'm getting a bit fed up with her. Always finding excuses to get me to her flat. Wants me to stay and talk to her, and then gets annoyed when I refuse. Wanted me to have a drink with her yesterday evening, silly old bitch. Why doesn't she act her age, instead of fluttering her eyelashes and trying to be coy. She gets under my skin. Otherwise it's all a doddle, and I've done a lot of good work on my speeches from here. Crowds are swelling with the silent police still pretending to be ordinary people. I wonder why they can't assess the situation better. I'm not anti-the realm in any way. I want a silent revolution for change, change from the inside of people. I want less aggressive thinking, for more harmony man between man. I won't advocate bomb dropping, terrorism or the like. But I won't accept corruption, or the so-called truth based on lies which is fed to the public through the media.

He was boiling the kettle for his mid afternoon coffee when the Manager appeared.

"Hello, sir. Haven't seen you for ages. Nothing wrong I hope. It's usually bad news that brings employer and employee together. You've left me to my own devices for so long that I thought everything was going well. Not coming to offer me a rise are you?" he added jokingly.

"No, not that." The Manager seemed embarrassed. There was only one chair in the cubby hole, so both men stayed standing.

"Have a cuppa?" asked Jon. "It's only black, can't be

bothered with milk. Goes off so quickly in this stuffy place."

The Manager raised his eyebrows a fraction. "No thanks, no coffee. The matter of fact is," and he paused. "Well, it's like this. The Ambassador's wife in the top flat is missing some money. She's quite sure she left it in her bag in her hall. She says you came in, and while you were there she went into the kitchen for something. She says no one else had been to the flat. She's very upset and thinks the Ambassador will be angry when he gets back tonight. She asked me if there was any way that there could be a check put on the property quickly. It's an embarrassing position I'm in," the Manager saw Jon's eyes harden and his lips tighten. "She's not actually saying you've taken it, but she's making it pretty obvious that she's pointing the finger at you."

"That damned old bitch," Jon exploded. "I'll tell you what's been happening. That whore has kept asking me to her flat under the most flimsy of pretexts. I had a cup of tea once, then never again, as I guessed what she had in mind. She painted her face and minced around and tried to make a pass at me. Because I refused a drink yesterday the old cow has turned sour. Concocted this little story. I'll be damned. I'll have you know, sir, that I will not stand by and be accused. I am going to leave this minute, and will call at the office tomorrow for my wages. You can explain what you like to the Ambassador. He might as well know what a tart he has married."

The Manager started to mutter, the problem was well beyond him. "It's O.K.," said Jon, "I know you can't deal with a situation like this. So just go back to work, and advertise for another janitor." Jon started to pack his holdall and hooked his overall on the peg. "Sorry it's got to end like this. Most of the job suited me well. But there isn't a job that's too good to leave if principles are involved. I'll say good day, sir, and I hope you will sort this matter out to your satisfaction. There's no way I could touch that woman's money. Please give that message to the

Ambassador. Goodbye sir." With a brief touch of his cap, Jon turned and climbed the stairs. The Manager, ill equipped as he was in these matters, went slowly to confront the Ambassador and his wife.

Jon started to walk. It was still only early afternoon, and he had a long evening ahead of him without the usual work. As the evening drew in, he slipped into a tiny cafe off the Kings' Road, and ordered tea and a bun. He slid into a narrow space by a long thin table scarcely looking at the customer on the other side.

"You look a bit glum" said a croaky high pitched voice. Jon looked up and saw a wizened old man with white hair going yellow, gaps between his teeth, and the brightest pale blue eyes that seemed on fire. His army great coat was many sizes too big for him.

"Not too bad," Jon replied. "Just given myself the sack after being accused of stealing."

"What's wrong with stealin'? Wouldn't be 'ere if it wasn't for a bit on the side." From the old man's accent Jon could tell he was from across the waters, the emerald isle. "Look at me, not much of me left, is there?" The old man grinned. "Been in the front line in two World Wars, and 'ere I am left with nothing. Cross my 'eart, this is my last cup o' tea for me. My pal, he's eighty five, I'm only eighty. We had a bit of a shindy last night in yon bar. Young 'uns were laughing at us. They noo we were in the wars and were proud of it. They said they'd never fire a gun at another man, and that we were murderers. Albert, that's my pal, I'm Arthur. Well, Albert, he got all worked up and threw his mug at the gang. Four of them set on old Albert, hit him mighty awful. Nose was bleedin', glasses broken. Then they scarpered. Had to get Albert to hospital. The boss at yon pub called a taxi, and we emptied our pockets. Taximan took one look at Albert, and said he'd take us whatever the cost. Albert's still there. Lucky bugger, broken nose and all, getting three meals a day. I've got to wait till Monday for the money. But," and Arthur leaned his small frame across the table. "Albert and me, we've gotta place to sleep."

"Well, that's something, " Jon nodded approvingly. He was beginning to admire this tough little dosser.

"It's not bleedin' Buckingham Palace. And I'm not really wanted. I know, you come wiv me. I'll show you the set-up. Rum place, it is. All going on underneath the house of God. He'd turn in His grave, or fall off his Throne, if He could see it. Come along now. It's getting dark. You can have Albert's place. Nothin' to pay. His Lordship up there is footin' the bill."

Arthur skuttled rather than walked down several minor roads. "My, you move fast for an eighty-year old," laughed Jon striding out to keep up.

"'ad to," Arthur chortled, "Moving fast's saved my skin several times. There's us that live like this, keepin' out of the way is what it's all about. Not like them young 'uns. Drawing attention to themselves, flashy this, flashy that. If I'd money in me pocket what they spend on their looks, I wouldn't be sleepin' in this bleedin' place."

Arthur led Jon down a cobbled path overgrown with shrubbery. A large red bricked church was on one side, and a square red bricked house down the other.

"That's where they come to say sorry for what they're goin' to do down below. They 'ave to appear up there sometimes. All part of the bargain." Arthur waved his arm towards the church. "Preacher lives in there, with his wife." He pointed to the red house. "Funny man, 'e must be blind and deaf. 'E's certainly not dumb."

As Arthur opened a wooden door, noise assailed them, loud high voices mingled with pop music. They went down a wide spiral staircase into an old room, it was a large square shape with a low ceiling. "This is the crypt," explained Arthur. "The Preacher 'as opened it for young people who 'e thinks are 'omeless. Rubbish that is in most cases. They pay a few pence a night, get free hot drinks, and the Preacher turns a blind eye to anythin' that they bring in. Drink flies about like it was a pub. Some of 'em stay all night coupling on the floor, all in public, just like wild animals. Preacher thinks it's good for them to have a roof, rather than sleeping rough. Ah, 'ere 'e is."

A portly gentleman, with egg down the front of his black cassock, approached the two men. "Evenin', Preacher. This is my friend. He's comin' for one night. Albert has met wiv some friends. That O.K. by you, Preacher?" The Preacher offered Jon a limp hand, there were two heavy gold rings on two of his fingers. He smelt of port. Jon said nothing, but took the hand briefly. He felt more and more uncomfortable yet interested at the outcome of his situation.

In an oily voice the Preacher said, "Good evening, Arthur. May you and your friend sleep well, and thank our gracious Lord for his goodness."

"Bullshit," muttered Jon under his breath. The two older men watched the crowd of young people, laughing, drinking, cursing and making love.

"This is supposed to be a young people's club. It's just a bloody brothel. No supervision except for that gold ringed drip. What's he doing it for? Get a good mark up for a large congregation? God, it makes me sick. How did you get in here, all of eighty?" Jon asked angrily.

Arthur twinkled. "We Irish can spin a good yarn, don't forget. Promised we'd acknowledge our sins, and spread the word along the road of Preacher's good works. Give up my sins? My foot, I'd rather die. Me money goes on me whisky, and even then there's not enough either of money or whisky. I've worked hard all me life. Not like some of them in there. They don't know what 'ard work is, I say. Preacher said Albert and me could doss down in passage. The crypt was for the young. We're not allowed to sleep in the crypt. Got a rug and a cushion each hidden behind the curtain."

Arthur poked behind a large thick curtain. He produced the bedding, and proudly laid it down along the side of the wall opposite the door. He managed to keep a silent dignity. "Got to stay along the wall. Youngsters come along this passage to toilet."

With an effort the old man lay on the rug, pulling half of it over his body and over his head. Soon he was snoring. Jon stayed sitting up, his arms around his knees.

Just then a group of inebriated youth charged through the door and along the passage to the toilet. They bumped along Arthur's sleeping form, having no regard for the old man. It made Jon angry.

What a God damned awful place! An old man of eighty left to sleep in the passage, the young drinking and goodness knows what in the warm.

When they returned he called out, "Mind your feet there. You know that the old man sleeps in this passage. Give him his due respect. I'd like to walk over you lot when you're fast off. Just to show you what it's like." The youngsters, all still in their teens, either stuck out their tongues or raised their two first fingers. Jon did not sleep that night.

Directly Arthur woke up, Jon said, "Come on now, we're off to have something to eat."

"I told you last night, I'm skint. I'll just have to wait for the charity of the Preacher. Cup of tea this evening, and maybe a sandwich or two."

"Don't you believe it," Jon replied. "Today I'm going to see you get a proper meal. I haven't enough money now to buy you one, but you meet me at that little cafe this afternoon, and I'll see what I can do. It makes me boil to see the way you are treated."

"Don't fash yourself, young man," said Arthur. "I'm still alive. What do I care what them scums think? They don't 'urt me, they only 'urt themselves. But I'll be there, this a'rternoon."

Jon rose to pavement level, glad to have left last night's sordid scene. He had to have instant work, just four hours work to raise the cash for two lunches. He would be alright himself when he had collected his wages from the flats but late afternoon was a long way off.

He walked towards the city, first King's Road, and then across to the Fulham Road, asking for work along the way at the small cafes as they were opening. He came to a large place on a corner, chairs and tables already on the pavement. Breakfasts were being served. He went in, and approached a foreign man behind the desk. After moments of wild gesticulations and play acting Jon gathered he was accepted, and was to start immediately behind the scenes, washing up and clearing the tables. He was shown a row of dirty white aprons, it appeared there were several absentee staff.

"What's happened to everybody else?" he ventured to ask a man, sweating heavily over the frying pan.

"Some coming later. You go work. Quick, quick. I no stop to talk. I want coffee, I want hot milk, I want clean plates. Now quick, quick."

"So that's the game," thought Jon. "Staff coming in late. I'm on my own. Well, here goes." He toiled and toiled, washing, clearing, stacking, to and fro, to and fro. He saw some other staff arriving at various times.

At ten o'clock the cook called, "Vot for breakfast? And boiling water now. Quick. Boiling water."

"Bacon sandwich, please. With coffee." Jon expected a short lunch break and was exceedingly hungry. After half an hour cook said again, watching with a smile the mountains of crockery, jugs, silver ware, glass ware and cutlery that were piling up, "Vot for breakfast? Vere is my boiling water?" Jon took no notice, keeping his hands busy. He heard a chanting from the other employees. "No bacon for the staff, no bacon for the staff." He reckoned he was being ridiculed as he was the only British worker, and the others were waiting for his reactions. He kept his cool but slid a pan of cold water along the cooker top.

"Vere is my boiling water?" asked the cook angrily when

he saw the cold water.

"Where is my bacon sandwich? You gave me nothing, so go and get the blinking hot water yourself." Jon's quick retort brought smirks from the junior staff. It seemed a battle had been won, for a large sized bacon sandwich appeared at the double. At the end of the shift Jon had enough money for a hot lunch with Arthur. It was the last time he met the old man, dosser exemplary. He walked to the Manager's office and collected his wages, and felt a free man again.

That night, sitting under a light at Victoria Station, he felt depressed. The thought of Arthur, the sight of his fellow dossers flitting round the station trying to look occupied and trying to find a bedding down place, and the incomprehension on the faces of some of his audience in the Park all made a sense of hopelessness flood over him. He wrote in his pad.

```
Why has this moment of depression assailed me when
last week I felt like a million dollars?      I use
my breath only for breathing and speaking, I can
claim I have the very earth under my feet, I could
claim I was marking time and taking stock, but in
reality I appear to be doing nothing.  Have I joined
the masses who have lost interest in life?      Is my
outlook reduced by the discomfort it gives to my
senses or has the heavy weight of hypocrisy become
part of my own diet?      I have stopped applauding
argument erectors as they brilliantly demolish their
hypothetics with mental gymnastics. Has silence ceased
to become productive and just become dumb insolence?
Or is it my inner weariness, the continual effort
to keep clean, to sleep, to eat, to keep warm, that
gives me a feeling of impotence when I survey the
social climate around me?     But as I am a servant
of divine principle I must leave myself open to the
influence of the Supreme Intelligence.      Lifemanship
not only requires an increasing self containment, but
it demands the ability to overcome physical hardship.
If standards are lowered by accepting social diplomacy
then awareness is harder to find, and before awareness
```

is re-won we wallow in negatives and lose opportunities
to elevate human denigration. I must look for areas
of tolerance to allow lifemanship to work... Forward...
enough of brooding.

That night Jon walked down to the Embankment and along to Waterloo Bridge. It was well past midnight when he arrived and he could find no spare box for his night's rest. He propped himself against an archway, and dropped in and out of a light doze. The birds had started to sing when Jon heard the sound of a heavy lorry coming towards him.

It's that damned council again. Washing the road down. The blighters seem to turn the water on faster when they come to the sleeping bodies under the bridges. Then they laugh back at the down and outs who yell their anger, their sleep broken. Reminds me of my dungeon cell, in Poland during the war. Middle of winter, starving I was, and covered in lice. Doing ninety days solitary after an escape. Warders hated me. Threw cold water over my cell floor every morning, and laughed when it froze and I slipped. Only had a thin sweater and two thin blankets. These buggers get the same sadistic pleasure, safe in their truck..

He approached the vehicle. He called up to the driver. "Hi, there. Couldn't you do this later on in the day? Sleep is hard enough for these poor buggers to find without you coming along and waking them up. It's too wet for them to doss down again when you've gone."

"Orders is orders, and that lot shouldn't be here anyway. Just a nuisance they are. I'd be glad to keep them off the street altogether." The driver spoke with a cigarette hanging out of his mouth, he seemed rolled in fat, fat on his chin, the back of his neck and his hands.

"When have you been uncomfortable? Never, I should say. You're covered in fat from over-eating. Can't you begin to understand the difficulties of these fellows, they're already tragically handicapped by their conditions. Why not start your cleaning at seven or eight in the morning in places where there are sleeping people?"

"Fuck off," shouted the driver, and he started up his vehicle, making the pressure of water even greater. Jon's legs and boots got a soaking. "You're completely inhuman," shouted Jon, but the noise of the machinery drowned his words. He watched silently as the vagrants tried to collect their sodden bits of belongings. His heart went out to them, there was so little he could do.

CHAPTER TEN

Movements in Summertime

It was the first Sunday in May and Jon planned his speech in the Park to coincide with the May Day holiday, and anticipating that it might prove provocative he promised himself a breakfast to sustain himself for the output of adrenalin he would have to use. He walked through the Park towards the lakeside restaurant: it was still early, and the dew was fresh, the leaves looked innocent in their newness, and the ducks looked broody. The tranquillity of the scene was rudely shattered when a youth walked towards him. He was dirty, long hair knotted, trousers tied with an old tie, and out of his coat pocket peered a greeny coloured bottle.

"Morning, sir. Gotta tanner, have you?" The young man spoke in an educated voice. His breath stank and his eyes were full of despair.

"No, I've not got a tanner. You'd only spend it on more of that damned stuff," said Jon pointing to the bottle. "But you can come with me and we'll have a mighty good breakfast."

"Seems I can't hold myself together," said the young man in reply to Jon's questions. "Did well at school, but never had friends. Couldn't seem to mix. I came to London, thinking it would be easy. Looked pretty good then. But I couldn't seem to hold a job, always wanted something else. Kind of grass greener in someone else's field. I wasn't drinking then. Now it seems it's all that keeps me going. Vicious circle I'm in... I drink and I'm a mess, and no one will employ me, and when I can manage to tidy up I can't seem to find work anymore. I know I'm for the rubbish tip, and when I'm sober that scares me."

The youngster talked continuously till they arrived at the restaurant. Jon guided him to a seat and went to order what he could afford. While he was waiting to be served he glanced around and watched the looks of disapproval of the customers at the state of his guest. Two of them moved across to the far side of the room; Jon collected his order, and went to sit with the young man.

"Not too bad," laughed Jon. "Couldn't make it stretch any further. I'm looking for work too, over twenty jobs I've tried for during this last weekend. Been turned down at the lot, some because of my age and some obviously because of my appearance but they didn't actually say that. Now eat up, young man. This will help, even if only for a moment."

"I'm mighty grateful, sir. But don't the dirty looks that these people give me make you feel bad? I feel I was something the cat brought in. 'Spose it's the bottle and my untidy hair. God! What would my parents think if they knew I was like this?"

"Isn't that a good enough reason to get yourself together?" asked Jon. He was not going to give the youngster a sermon.

"Some days I think I'll manage, then I buy another bottle just to help me on, and so it goes. But sir, it's done me the world of good just to be accepted for what I am. Thanks for that, and for the grub." Jon kept the conversation light, the youth knew himself well, it was up to him and him only to get straight. An outsider could not give advice. They soon left the restaurant, and Jon walked towards Speaker's Corner.

The crowd on his patch were waiting. Jon got his step ladder. Slowly he began.

"May Day has just gone and all the celebrations are over for the year. Now I am going to talk about the state of the Soviet Union, that so-called communist state. Funny sort of communism, everything dictated from the top. Where is the equality? Where is the right for the peasant to speak out?"

"Bleedin' same 'ere. No one listens to shop floor or people with nuffink in pockets."

"Who makes the rules? Just the small and powerful minority sucking like leeches the life blood of the poor, and who grab for more and more power and authority?"

"Don't 'ave to go furver than nose to find tha'" Jon paused, determined not to be put off his theme. "I am told that the fishes have to move aside because of Russian submarines. I am told that millions of people are hungry while guns come before butter, before freedom. If that kernel of autocrats in power do not relax their grip on the people, and if the liberalisation that Kruschov has tried to put into practice is thwarted then the USSR will not survive in world opinion. We know their concentration camps are full, we know that geniuses are given psychiatric treatment by morons whose sole job is certifying. We know that thousands are wrongly imprisoned. We know that thousands join the KGB and so become exempt from human service. We know that the Jews live in fear, fear of betrayal, fear of programs. But you cannot douse the spirit of the simple Russian people. One day these people, those in the Soviet Resistance, will create a climatic freedom, the Latvian, Lithuanians, the Estonians and the people in concentration camps will be rid of the ruthless power of the hammer and sickle. The Soviet Dictatorship will be overthrown in one decade. The thousands of Jews will be free of persecution and will be able to go to worship their God and retain their own culture in Israel. Men wrongly imprisoned will be released. Communications with the West will be re-assumed. Fellow citizen will trust fellow citizen.

"Having said all that, what next? What about us here?" an interruption wailed from his left.

Jon stuck to his point. "That is the situation told briefly. I can tell you more. But there are other similar cases, where dictatorship, oppression and denigration of the individual occur. I call on you all to oppose these tyrannies, where man is manipulated, where human progress is not only retarded but obstructed, where the individual does not count as an individual, only as a number. You say, what about us here? Some say that you can do nothing. I say you can. Talk about oppression, write about oppression. On your doorsteps watch out for cases where the individual is not given due respect, young or old. Speak out against tyrannies where man is brain-washed, influenced by subtle dogmas and slogans. We must all stop human progress from being retarded or obstructed."

Jon stayed on his ladder and fielded questions, some were loaded with anger, some proved threatening. The silent policemen seemed to move closer, they were watching the battle of words. Before Jon left his step ladder he called out, "those whose job it is to watch for the safety of this country, and who are here time and time again in disguise, will see who among this lot," and he waved his hand over the heads of the crowd, "you will see from this lot those who are patriots of our country, and those who have the power to undermine and divide. I leave it to you, gentlemen, what will you do?" He packed up the ladder and quickly left the gathering, some angry voices shouting after him.

The adrenalin that surged through his veins after his speech soon drained away and once again he took to the road and walked to Covent Garden, to the small cafe open round the clock.

"Cuppa, please," he asked the owner, a cheerful old type London cockney.

"Anythin' t'eat?" asked Bill, his cap turned round backwards, spotted scarf twisted round his neck.

"Not today, thanks. I'm a bit skint. But, my goodness, you've no idea what it means to us to know that you're always open. Over these months you've been a life-line."

"'ave a banger, on tick," offered Bill. "We know yer well enough. Know yu'd square up in th'end."

"Sure I would. Wouldn't leave a bad debt. Jobs don't grow on trees for my age group. Thanks a lot, mate, thanks a lot." He took his mug and banger and found a vegetable crate and sat in a corner well away from the bustling crowd. Being Sunday they were mostly flower sellers at small stalls. Amongst the sellers and buyers were those who, like himself, had nowhere to go, but who unlike himself had nothing to do.

Work, work, work, top of my list is paid work. I won't try any more pubs as I think the youngsters from the colleges are filling those gaps. I've a hunch I will get a place at the ITV headquarters. Will try there tomorrow. Then I could kill two birds with one stone, earn money and find out the kind of person who controls the domestic air power and manipulates the minds of the public.

Just look at those people's faces. Shuffling around, eyes down, deadpan expressions. They seem soul dead, moving statues of boredom. How do they inwardly deal with endless boredom?

Tucked in his corner, and comfortable on his box Jon took out and wrote in his pad, a pad that was rapidly filling up with poems, statements to bring to mind passing thoughts of philosophies, and notes for the backbone of speeches.

```
Fear of boredom is like being scared of the dark.
We continue to pretend to serve the Goddess of eternal
youth, until we see through the deception of pretence
and we start to lose composure at the oncoming piles
of nothingness.  Instead desperation causes us to
feel insecure, and in the clutches of desperation
we lack the ability to be able to fulfil our needs,
so we wallow in boredom.  The enemy of boredom is
the bottle or the needle, and both being readily
available we reach for one of them.  Amongst the
droning decibels of noise of so called fashionable
music, we admit to self inadequacy, none of the standards
imposed during the previous years being reached or
maintained.  But even at this level of nothingness
there are things we cannot accept or dare not reject.
```

At this moment need and the birth of acceptance come together, making a way for awareness. This awareness can start the search for truth, a seed sown in nothingness. Now can begin our start in lifemanship. The extrovert and loneliness are exchanged for aloneness, with self sufficiency. The helplessness of a cuddly teddy bear is rejected. We start to wonder at the influence of phallic dependence, and declare that we need no longer become its daily wounded casualty. We realise that the pastime between the thighs is no passport to joy, only a fragmented moment of pleasure which often has costly side effects. We are starting to know that we have to help ourselves. Advice, manipulations, emotional blackmail can come from all quarters, from friends, counsellors, the media, the religionists, but it is ourselves that have to sift out the right course for ourselves. For any journey undertaken for the wrong reasons is doomed to failure. But why am I writing 'we'? Perhaps it is my deepest wish that these poor sad futureless wanderers could be embraced in that thinking. Then they would have a spark of hope.

Finding work is more and more difficult. Perhaps it's Life's way of telling me that no action can be more profitable than action. To do or not to do, that is not the question, nor does the answer lie in just manipulating, or performing a function to keep up with those who believe that to conform to the majority gives a rightness to the cause.

Jon put his pad away, and sat still, statue like.

*God damn it, it's nine months since I left home. Am I on the right track? It's just such hard work keeping going, to find any sort of roof over my head is a time consuming problem. Light, heat and warmth is free at Rolling Stock Hotel, but the cost of getting there is enormous. It's hard to concentrate on an empty stomach, can't really think constructive thoughts. Don't even crave for a cigarette any more. **That** was a hurdle well taken. I've kept pretty well so far, except for my feet, and a nasty looking rash inside*

*my groin. 'Spose that's the pee blowing back at me when
I am outside, and I've nothing to dry off on. Could get
quite sore if I don't take care... Am I cutting myself off
from people, I don't mean my family, just every sort of people?
That can be the downfall for a revolutionary like myself
looking for change. Maybe I try too hard to help if people
are hurt by social demands but my efforts are like a grain
of sand in the desert. Maybe that one grain will help to
support a great palm. Wonderful thought.*

"'i, there old cock." Bill's face loomed before Jon's eyes, bringing him back with a jolt from his mental roamings. "Yer bin 'ere so long, thought yer were a statue. Writin' away in that there pad. Cuppa on the slab for yer. Never seen un sit so still. Thought yer were a gonner."

"I've a long way to go yet," laughed Jon, his limbs creaking with the effort of standing up. "Backbone of London, you are. You're always cheerful, and seem to know exactly what's going on. Wish there were more like you. Cockneys seem a dying breed."

"That's right, mate. Wha's good enough for us, ain't good enough for young 'uns. You 'ear my Bertha. She right blows off wot they're doin' to our street. Blocks of flats 'ere, blocks of flats there. There be no more talkin' on doorsteps. No more poppin' out for a cuppa. It's all change, rushin' 'ere, rushin' there, and wot for? If these young 'uns," he pointed to the figures roaming round, "if these young 'uns 'ad stayed 'ome and worked nearby they'd not be like they are. Given ideas by tha' bloody box. 'ere you are, mate, 'ave a sandwich. Plenty cut, and it's Sunday. Shouldn't get many coming tonight. Me brother comes at ten. There must be a cuppa for them that wants 'un."

"You're worth a million," said Jon. "I'll square you up with a bonus one day. I can accept a cuppa from you, as you make me feel there are no strings attached. When a charity hands one out the Lord has to be praised or some such. I even had a prayer leaflet shoved in my hand the other day."

Bill burst out laughing. "Yer've got yer own ideas. Keep goin'. Cum agin an' see me."

The rest of Sunday passed by slowly. Jon spent the start of the night at Waterloo, sitting on a bench. The railway police came marching by, flashlights flailing. "Move on, you there, move on. Not you again, don't want any cheek from you." The uniformed man started to look even more aggressive.

Jon replied, this time somewhat mildly, "you've helped me to learn one thing. I value what little sleep you lot allow me now I'm sleeping rough, and it makes the sleep I had when I had a bed seem of poor value and quite unappreciated. Wish you'd realise sleep was more important than food. You wouldn't be so eager to wake us all up. But we all know that the likes of you do not have an inkling how it feels not to have. May you all rot in your own beds!"

"That's enough. Move on, and out of here quick."

"Can't go quick, you fool. My legs are numb. But I'm off in my own time, don't you worry." Jon hobbled out of the precinct towards the city. Tired as he was after three hours sleep he stayed on Waterloo Bridge to watch the sunrise. The water moving slowly and sluggishly played games with itself, the ripples seemingly wanting to stay in night time shades, the orange glow of the dawning sun slowly winning by painting out the darker colours. The black silhouettes seemed defiant in the darkness, then as the sun rose above the horizon they too took on the challenge of daylight. Noise was muted save for the sea gulls, those wild fishermen now known as town scavengers, screaming for their breakfast. This brief respite into the world of nature brought balm to Jon's soul and he silently thanked the policeman for disturbing his night.

After a big wash and brush up in the toilets, cleaning his shoes with toilet paper and water, he felt he looked passable. He walked slowly to the ITV headquarters, up the stairs, and again asked to see the Personnel Manager.

Hope they don't hear my tummy rumbling, I'm so God darned hungry. Perhaps they'll give me a cuppa.

To appear less of a wanderer he left his precious holdall in the care of the Hall Porter and received a disc in return. The Personnel Manager was a middle aged man, who seemed to fall between conforming to convention and being a little off-beat. He had shoulder length hair, which sat oddly in his role, he wore a collar and tie, but with a leather jacket covered with badges. He had grey trousers of an old fashioned cut, and brown suede shoes. Both men seemed to have good feelings for each other and the Manager immediately offered Jon a job in the kitchens, doing the vegetables and clearing the tables. Again he was on the bottom of the ladder, but he nicknamed himself a potato surgeon, and laughed to himself.

"You can start straight away," said the Manager. "Your boss will be Matilda. She's black, but she's a good sort. If you work well, you'll get on with her. I have a feeling you might be able to give her a bit of moral support. You can feed in the canteen, the rates are much reduced for staff. Hope this suits you."

"I'll give it a go," Jon replied, determined to hide his eagerness to get near some food and hot drink. This time he was given a clean white overall. Having been shown the geography of the canteen, the kitchen, the recreational room, and of course, the toilets, Jon was introduced to Matilda, then the Manager left for his other duties. Matilda was the roundest, blackest woman Jon had ever seen, with the thickest lips giving the widest smile he had ever received. She spoke beautiful English in a deep mellow voice.

"Hello," she said, "can't shake hands with you, look at this flour up to my elbows. You've just come at the right moment. Look at that pile of veg to be tackled before the dinner hour. Last lad left yesterday, can't think why he wasn't happy. He wasn't a streak of lightening anyway, maybe he won't find work as easily as he thinks. But you're no lad," Matilda looked at Jon, her merry eyes quizzical. "Knives are in this drawer," and she pointed to a cupboard. "When I'm free of the flour I'll make you a how-do-you-do cup of tea. We're a bit pushed till the lunch hour is over."

True to her word, a large mug of tea arrived shortly. Jon beavered away with the vegetables. Then miraculously a huge plate of thick sandwiches appeared. "Do you mind working through the lunch break? We're so behind hand with the lad going without notice," Matilda asked anxiously.

"Of course I don't mind," said Jon with a laugh. "And if you blink your eyelids just once you'll find all the sandwiches gone." He wolfed down the food, glad to feel his hunger a bit abated.

"My, that was quick," said Matilda. "Have a feeling it's some while since you ate." Another plate of sandwiches arrived. "Make your first day a treat day, won't happen again," said Matilda with a twinkle. Jon could guess that she had the treasured ability to assess need when the need was real, a gift that those who live near to the grass roots of life seem to acquire.

Jon worked the middle shift, ten am till six or seven pm. It suited him very well. There were good toilet facilities, and he was able to keep himself remarkably clean and tidy, and could tend to the angry rash on his groin. He even managed to wash a few clothes, putting them in a plastic bag till the evening time, and then drying them in the warm night air. Summer certainly had its compensations for those whose bedroom embraced the heavens. He asked to be paid daily till he could save up enough to last a week, and then he went on weekly payments. Soon he was promoted from vegetable boy to domestic duties in the restaurant itself. He collected the dirty items, emptied ashtrays, and cleaned the floor and tables. As a member of staff he was able to use the bar to which all members of the Headquarters were allowed. Without his white coat, and as neat and tidy as he could be, he looked little different from the other staff. He talked with anyone he could, always questioning, always probing, often promulgating his concepts for the need for change. He felt this was a very fertile area for his ideas.

One evening he was drinking on his own, stoking up before embarking on his night time's hassle. A heavily built, well dressed man approached him.

"Evening, Jon," said the Director. "Mind if I sit here? Sorry for calling you by your Christian name, but I don't know your other one."

"To begin with," said Jon prickly, "Jon is not my Christian name, for I am not a Christian. It is however my first name. Secondly, I don't mind a bit where you sit. As you well know free seats are available to anyone. I know you're the Director of this set up, so what do you want of me?"

That's not a very good beginning, thought the Director. Wonder why he's so defensive. Aloud he said, "Hope you're O.K. here. Matilda is a tower of strength isn't she? How come, though, you are doing this kind of job?"

"I don't ask you how come you are doing your kind of job, do I?" Jon seemed really aggressive.

"Don't want to rattle you, Jon. Won't ask you any more questions. But some of the staff have heard you speaking in the Park, and they like what you say. They were, and I was to, wondering why you are here? I'm sure I could use some of your ideas on the media. Have you any thoughts of doing anything different."

"Sorry I was abrupt sir," Jon replied. "I feel people are always trying to get me to do something I don't want to do, and with money usually as the carrot. Thanks for the offer, I am sure it was meant kindly, but I don't want to feel manipulated, and that is partly why I am where I am."

"But you're wasted, peeling potatoes and clearing the tables.

It makes me angry to see such talent going unused. In fact, if I catch you in the kitchen in a month's time," and then the Director laughed, "I'll punch you on the chin."

"And if you offer me promotion, I shall leave," replied Jon quickly. Both men were laughing, and they struck up a happy relationship, and drank late into the night. When the Director looked at his watch he was aghast.

"Gosh, I'm late. Must phone my missus. She is used to me arriving home at unexpected hours. Have you far to go?" he asked.

"Not too far and not too near," replied Jon evasively. The Director was not listening, and they parted after a rapid handshake, Jon to his trees and grass under the sky and the Director to his well appointed home. Like the other staff, the well paid, well dressed Director did not dream that his fellow drinker, complete with collar and tie, could be sleeping at Cardboard Hall.

Matilda was a joy to Jon. She worked very hard and ran the kitchen and the restaurant with great skill and zeal. In spite of her excellent English she was ridiculed and mimicked, and Jon was able to go to her defence. One evening she took Jon to her home and introduced him to her family, tall black husband, and two bonny bouncing black teenagers. He had a wonderful evening, they lavished Barbadian hospitality on him, and he relaxed in the warmth of family unity. But he felt a vacuum in his own heart, a sudden yearning for the hustle and bustle of his other life. He acknowledged this yearning and suppressed it as quickly as he could. Without questioning, Matilda always left food on a plate for him which he could either eat as he worked, or wrap up for the evening hours. He was glad to see her every day.

If the recreation room was quiet he would slip in there for an hour to write in his pad, if it was occupied he wrote under the stars by lamplight if he was sober enough. Most evenings he went to one of his favourite pubs, and put the liquid gun to his head, a necessary evil of escapism for him.

The landlord of the Jug and Bottle used to be a well known wrestler, and he collected odd customers around him from all parts of the world, paying customers with individual tendencies he called them. Jon liked this joyful publican who managed to keep unwanted disturbances to the minimum on his premises. However brief their dialogue was to each other both held a silent respect for each other's position.

One evening two very attractive women stood at the bar. Although they were not regulars the landlord made a great fuss of them, blatantly ogling at the taller blonde. Jon stood and watched, mesmerised by the femininity of the striking women.

It's a long time since I've been close to such sexual attraction. Wonder if I'll get a rise on? Just look at those breasts and long, long legs. No, nothing's happening, nothing stirring. Damn it, am I losing all sexual feelings 'cos I'm living rough? Not old enough for that. Wonder if it happens to other dossers. Haven't spoken to them about it.

The experienced landlord made it easy for Jon to be accepted in the conversation. "We're both actresses," said the blonde. "But can you guess, we're resting!" And they laughed nervously. "In other words we haven't got an acting job."

"But," said her friend, long black hair twisting sensuously down to her waist. "I'm lucky to be able to earn some money." The landlord was called to another customer, so Jon was the only listener to the two women. "It's the most God-darned awful boring job. I teach fat business men how to make speeches so that they can make more money to make themselves even fatter. I hate every moment of it, but we need the money. They don't seem to think I'm an ordinary person with ordinary feelings. I can't help my face and figure, and I've got to look good as that is all part of my bread and butter. Can't stop them pawing me at every possible moment. They know I've been on the stage and this seems to give them the idea I'm on the sex market. Just like it is when you're a widow."

She looked at her friend, her lovely blonde friend. Jon saw in both their beautiful faces a tired expression which reflected the weariness of spirit, the blonde was wearing a wedding ring. He felt quite paternal towards them both, an older man in sympathy with youth.

"It's hard at times," replied Jon, "specially in a world where standards are getting lower and lower. But there's one thing you've got to remember, and this may help. There are many of us compelled to pass through experiences and have to fight to keep our own identity. You are not alone."

When it was time to close, the actresses packed up to go. The blonde turned to Jon and said, "thank you for giving me courage to go on."

Jon was a bit taken aback, but he replied, "I didn't give you courage. I only took away the things that were obscuring courage from yourself."

He felt glad that all three of them had, for a moment, shared a sense of soul, without strings. Once again he left his new found acquaintances to go to their homes, and he went to search for a box and an alleyway. As he pottered down the side streets off the Brompton Road he looked up at the sky. It was starless, it looked brooding and heavy with rain. Even the cats were darting here and there as if anxious to find their beds. At the top of three steps there were several boxes, mostly small. There were no lights on in the building and it appeared to be offices. Jon did the best he could with the boxes breaking some down to lie on, and covering himself with the rest. He even tried to make a wall of empty ones to stop him from being seen from the road. Then it started to rain, and it poured. Great drops seemed to attack him from every corner where the boxes left a gap. There was nothing he could do but ride it out, fortunately the problem of being soaked was not a calamity, just another occurrence that had to be accepted. Then the storm passed and suddenly the rain stopped. Jon stayed where he was, there was nothing better to do. Dawn had not yet started. While he dozed fitfully he heard a car, which screeched to a stop, then he saw the familiar beam of light.

"Move on, come on, get up. You'll be had for trespassing." A boot poked Jon under the buttocks. Although the invader had a peaked cap which Jon could see silhouetted against the sky Jon called out quickly.

"I'm getting up. But first show me your card. I want to know just who and what you are. I'm harming no one, I'm minding my own business, and I'm very, very wet. You know there will be nowhere to go for the rest of the night. Why can't you be more human and go and get a real burglar? I think it boosts your ego to take away what dignity we're left with. But you're probably so stupid you don't know what I am talking about." Jon was standing up now. "Where's this card I asked for? Your identity card?"

"Shut your trap, and shove off," was all the constable replied, and he hastily moved towards the car.

"O.K.," shouted Jon, "you don't show me your card. I can see the number of your car. Got plenty of time to go to the Station to report you."

"You piss off," shouted the constable banging the door. "If you give us more trouble, we'll make trouble for you." The car reversed and screeched off down the small road.

Ah, well! It takes all sorts to make a world. There are some good 'uns in the force. It's sad they deal with us like that. Cor, I'm soaked. Will swop my shirt and sweater with the ones from my bag. They'll dry off in the afternoon. Trousers will have to stay wet. Never mind. Pity about the sleep. Could've done with a few hours undisturbed. Now I'll just walk around keeping warm till daylight.

Completeness

Before the sun was ever a complaint
Or the moon too bright and full
Whether for lunatics or lovers
I saw many stars in childhood's dreams
Shoot it out with the universe.
What I knew was little and belief had not begun
For acceptance of reality outshone,
And 'being' was enough for me.
I saw and felt life's love,
So there was nothing left to prove.

Part Three

CHAPTER ELEVEN

The Attack

The summer months passed quickly. Jon stayed at the ITV Headquarters cleaning, scrubbing, polishing, clearing up, and Matilda glowed like the embers of a camp fire at night. With Jon around no one played her up. Jon became well and stayed well, the one meal a day and a regular routine more than compensated for his roofless existence. He spent his small wage on food and the endless rounds of drinks in the pubs which were still his haven in his non-working hours. He met many people in the ITV Headquarters, people of all colours, class and prejudices, and there was opportunity for him to expound his ideas. He still had a running battle with the disciplinary forces that a large city like London conjures up, he spoke from his ladder in the Park with regularity, his crowds getting bigger and more expectant. He kept himself as clean as he could, topping up his wardrobe with newer boots and a coat as winter approached. He was able to write in his pads poetry of his soul during the long summer evenings, and in the dawn before the city woke. His holdall, which he carried everywhere, was heavy with the weight of his written words, squeezed amongst his spare clothing. With the warmer weather his fellow dosser seemed more sprightly, as if they were able to put the thoughts of the rigours of another winter out of their minds. But the numbers of the under privileged and the homeless were increasing, the power of the media was entwining itself around the minds of young children, whole families, and so to communities, and the fleshpots of city life and unrealistic freedoms were persuasively depicted. Money was the present god to be worshipped, and to have money gave a new found status. Competition was rife with honesty a poor second. Drugs were filtering their ugly way into stratas of society that were innocent of their effects. The political situation in Ireland was an ever open sore, with the terrorist attacks a constant reminder. Jon spurred himself to continue to alert his fellow man to the oncoming dangers that he foresaw unless the thinking of society, from Governmental levels to those at the grass roots, could be revolutionised. While he was doing this he made friends and he made enemies, but, undaunted, he continued to press for the fundamental change he deemed so important first at the personal level, then at national level to save the authority of the country from being undermined, and then at international level. The task was enormous, but one day, someone whom he did not know upset the smooth running of his present mode of existence, and temporarily halted his self imposed mission.

The incident occurred one Sunday in late October in 1971 when he spoke again in the Park. The nights were lengthening, and the warm air of the summer months had changed to a brisk coldness and autumn frosts crisped the dawn. The fight against the forces of nature had begun, the circumstances of battle were unnatural, human beings sleeping on concrete, freezing in the cold and wet with none of the aids of the wild to use against the weather, aids like leaves, wood, burrows, or packed snow. Jon walked slowly across the Park, by-passing the restaurant, some instinct drove him to speak on an empty stomach. The crowds were already assembling at Speaker's Corner, they were hectoring a cleric who was labouring on about world poverty, extolling the listeners to send clothes or money to various charities. When parts of the crowd saw Jon they washed like a wave over to his plot. Slowly Jon collected his stepladder and erected it in its usual place near the Park's perimeter railings, he did not like to feel people were able to get behind him. He tucked his hold-all between the legs of the stepladder. Slowly he started to speak.

His theme was once again social change, he still did not call it revolution for that conotated violence. "I challenge you all," he continued, "in sensibilities name, to take a hand in fate rather than having fate thrust upon us by 'big brother'." There was heckling immediately from the fringes of the crowd, several of whom were in their usual state of inebriation. Then Jon turned his words towards the IRA.

"At each point of history where change might have come about, there are those of you who resist the change by means of force, not reason. Bombs are laid in places where and when it is known that women and children will pass by. Those of you in this organisation of destruction claim that you defend your country, but your unborn will come to realise that you were a lot of paranoids wishing nobody any good. They will not thank their fathers for causing death and destruction, for spreading anxiety and fear. The way you, the silent force of destruction, are discharging venom is without reason." At this moment Jon noticed a young man press to the front of the crowd and walk across from one side to the other. The man purposely kicked the foot of the stepladder. Jon managed to regain his balance, but he mentally assessed that the young man had kicked the steps to see if Jon has his quota of 'keepers', the silent men who are detailed to keep the peace and watch for insurrection. None of the stony faced men moved. Jon tried to assemble his thoughts but his thread was lost. He continued with practical matters.

"The bombs you place are supposed to demoralise our land. Our people will not change their minds or make decisions because of those savage attacks. And you try to play with fear, organising bomb hoaxes to disrupt the smooth running of our economy. It is here that the seedy side of politics plays into your hands, the editorials and television coverage giving the hoaxes a distorted importance, one political party playing against the other. You are trying to create an enemy within, a bogey of suspicion." The noise of disapproval of the crowd was growing more noticeable, some of them were swaying. Jon saw anxious faces of the camera-laden visitors, but still he continued.

"You who are responsible for deaths by violence are terrorists. You are putting back progress and are dividing brother from brother. How will you be remembered in the course of history?" These were the last words he spoke that Sunday.

He saw the same man who had bumped the stepladder move towards him again with the speed of an athlete. The man grabbed the rear part of the steps and projected Jon through the air as if he were throwing a two handed dart. With a squelch and a thud Jon landed on the long spiked railings that encircled the Park, and there he was impaled through both buttocks to the inside of the thigh, the weight of his body tearing the holes deeper and deeper. The crowd, now hypnotically attracted to the unfolding tragedy moved closer and closer. Jon managed to grasp the shoulder of one of the spectators, and slowly levered himself off the spikes. He stood up shakily, blood pouring from his legs and thighs.

"Best you lie down," he heard a woman's voice saying. "Best you lie down before you fall down. The ambulance will be here soon." Her calm voice gave Jon re-assurance so he lay face forward, on his stomach red pools forming either side of him, he was glad he could no longer hear the drip of his blood on the ground. As he lay his head was scuffed by a policeman's boot, as the policeman wrestled with the assailant, who was led away from the crowd yelling obscenities.

It's strange, I don't feel real pain, just numbness. I don't feel afraid, just terribly sad that this might be the end of everything. If I die all I ask is to be included in the graciousness of life itself. I don't want more... Why should he do that to me? Hope they keep that bastard.. Damn it, why are things going fuzzy? Can't seem to see much. It seems as if night is coming.

"Hi there, what's happening?" he called out in a hoarse whisper. He felt someone fumbling with his legs.

"It's alright, buddy," a foreign voice replied. "Don't you worry. Just relax. I've taken my tie off and I'm putting on a tourniquet. I'm a doctor, and this is the best I can do for the moment. You're losing too much blood to be left alone. The medics will take care of you when they come. Just lie still, and keep breathing. Try not to go to sleep."

Again Jon felt a moment of re-assurance, and with a flash to normality he re-called his work in his holdall. He croaked to the re-assuring voice, "My holdall. Find my holdall. It was under the steps." Then after a short pause he whispered, "it's all foggy, can't see anything, it's all..." and his voice trailed away. The crowd was slowly dispersing, some were in tears, many were white faced, they were all shaken. The ambulance siren sounded, and within seconds the vehicle arrived. With the efficiency of professionals they had Jon in the ambulance, still face down, motionless.

"Did you see all that blood?" asked one ambulance man. "He must be a gonner. Where shall we take him? Paddington St. Mary's."

The jolting when he was moved on to the stretcher had restored Jon into consciousness. Though he was lying still he heard what the man had said.

"Bugger me," Jon said huskily. "You bloody well take me to St. George's. I won't last the journey to St. Mary's, all of three miles. And I'm not a talking corpse either."

"Blimey, sir," said a more senior attendant. "You haven't half given us a fright. St. George's it will be, and top speed." The sirens started to wail. "Sorry sir, thought you'd copped it. We'll move in double-quick time. Very sorry sir." The attendant seemed upset.

Again Jon disappeared into the in-between world, and it was only when he was shaken on the shoulder by a white coated young doctor did he take stock of his situation. The ambulance crew had gone, and he was in a clinically clean small ward, lying on his back, tourniquet still in place.

The student doctor, standing by his bed, pad and pen in his hand, said coldly, "Next of kin?"

"That's out," retorted Jon. "I don't want formalities. You know my name. Surely that's enough? Get on with tying me up." He was convinced he was not going to pass bad news on to his family, specially as he had not given them good news for the past year.

"Your next of kin," repeated the student dully. He was now joined by another white coated man.

"We must have your next of kin," said the newcomer. Jon was becoming angry, and anger was as dangerous for him as fear was in the Park. The two students did not move.

"What are you doing to me?" asked Jon with eyes dimming again. "Surely you know that tourniquets cannot be held for too long. Get on with working on me. God, is there no one with any compassion?" He tried to look around the room and tried to lever himself off the trolley bed. The effort was great, but try as he could to move, he was too weak.

A slip of a girl appeared, a young uniformed VAD nurse. "I'm your friend," she told Jon, and briefly held his hand. "I've been watching what's happened. We'll get on with it now. You must relax and trust me." This small act of kindness gave Jon the will to live, a young nurse challenging bureaucracy and replacing officialdom with understanding. Even with his life's thread so delicately balanced Jon knew he would not submit to the doctor's questioning and make his family suffer more than they had suffered already from his departure. The nurse held the light like a slowly unfolding beacon of direction at the most crucial stage of a spaghetti-like junction. The two doctors were interested in the formalities, they did not identify with suffering. They would have let Jon die. The nurse knew it, Jon knew it and the doctors knew it too.

But now events began to move fast. The doctors removed

the tourniquets and applied clips. On their instructions the nurse administered the first injection, and Jon moving between enforced unconsciousness and normality was aware of her presence, and a sense of gratitude helped him to deal with his dilemma. The nurse then turned to the most delicate organs of his body and started to clean round them.

Still poised between life and death, the impishness of Jon's nature surfaced. "Take care of those," he said to the nurse, "I shall need them later." The two doctors overheard his words, and one of them lapsed into bogus self-righteousness.

"How dare you say that to the nurse?" he admonished.

The nurse was at the head of Jon's bed and managed to give his hand a slight squeeze. Nothing was said. Jon remained silent and his mind raced.

OK, you can hide behind respectability. But you've no idea the effort it took to create such coarse humour. All my dreams are on trial, and humour was part of my effort to fight this nightmare. Perhaps you were still able to smile inside? I hope so, for you have no escape from witnessing human tragedy, and the stress caused by this could crush the lighter side of life. But is it my fault that I am where I am? Have I been too naive? Is it the reality of my own nature, known and unknown, that has put me here? Whatever has led me to this point, I'm not giving up. I'm going to fight pain and despair with the power of thought until I die, or am so drugged I'm not in control. I am going to deny all human limitations.

Jon heard the two medics talking between themselves. An older grey-haired man joined them. He heard the words 'theatre and surgery'. The older man spoke softly and exuded an air of confidence.

The first young medic came to the bed-head and said in a subdued voice, "will you please sign this, sir. It only gives us your permission to operate."

After Jon had signed the form giving his permission for

surgery, the young man asked, "when did you last eat, sir? We always have to know this."

"You've nothing to worry on that score. I haven't eaten since yesterday."

"Thank you sir. Surgery is always best on an empty stomach."

Again Jon tried to relieve the tension with humour and with more spirit that belied his strength. "What are your political complexions, gentlemen?" he asked.

The young doctors ignored him, but the older man, a consultant, replied, "in this place we're all colours of the rainbow, and our patients, whether black, white, yellow or brown, are all given the same treatment. Just you rest now, we'll be operating to clean you up as soon as we can."

Jon was wheeled out of casualty, and into a side ward. The helpful nurse travelled with him. On the journey down the long corridors Jon remembered his holdall, and his heart thumped. "Nurse, nurse," he called. She was instantly at his head. "My holdall. Did my holdall come with me? Hope to God it did. Part of my life's work there. Tell me, nurse, did you see my holdall?"

"Don't worry, don't worry. The ambulance men gave it to the porter, who left it behind the Admittance Desk till they know what's going to happen to you. I'll see to it myself that it ends up in your ward. You may have to leave it with Sister when you're fixed up, but you'll know it is safe."

"God, you're wonderful. Better than all medicines. Where did you learn the art of understanding? Must have had to put up with a lot in your young life."

"You can say that again," the young girl answered. "Seen a lot of unhappiness. But you think of the good things that can happen tomorrow and all the other tomorrows. I'll come and see you when you've settled in, and I'll make sure your holdall is kept safe. Here we are. You won't be long before you go to theatre. I must off now, this is someone else's territory." Again the girl gave his hand a squeeze, a feeling of silent rapport passing between the two of them.

The preliminaries to a surgical operation began to take place. Another nurse injected him, he was wheeled on a long hard trolley down long hard passages, every movement hurting his torn flesh. Then into a clinical room where the masked anaesthetist peered over him. As the last knockout drops were administered Jon called out, hearing his voice coming from far away, "I'm depending on you to see you later." Then oblivion descended.

It took some time before Jon could drag himself from the in-between world. He slowly looked around him, there were tubes, bottles, white sheets, charts, and a clock, and a tap which was dripping. His breathing was dangerously shallow, and when he turned his head he saw blood on his pillow.

Must be in a state. Thank goodness I gave up smoking when I did. If I coughed now I think I'd die. God, I'm thirsty. I could drink a fountain. That bloody tap makes me thirstier than ever. I can't even call, my voice has dried away.

Eventually a starched Sister appeared to check on the various tubes and drips. She was not surprised to see that Jon was conscious. "May I have a drink please," he croaked.

"No," said the Sister firmly.

"I'm terribly thirsty."

"But you can't have a drink," she said firmly.

"Then I'll have to get one for myself. I can hear a tap not far away." Jon tried to lift his head, but even that was too much effort.

"Don't be childish," snapped the Sister, and walked away. She returned shortly with ice-cubes, and passed them across Jon's lips. "No patient is allowed fluid after an operation. You've had a long time under surgery, so you'd best behave. You're lucky to be here with us. The surgeon did a wonderful job. Now I suggest we co-operate. It would be easier for us both. OK?" The firm stern face broke into a smile. "OK," whispered Jon. "You win."

For two days Jon hovered between awakeness and half-sleep. He could do nothing for himself, and had to submit to the attentions of the nurses. He could feel the blood transfusions making him stronger. The first day he urinated and then, oh joy, on the second day his bowels opened. The pain was exquisite, but at least he knew his excretory areas were undamaged. The only other anxiety were his sexual organs. He smiled to himself when he found himself wondering how long it would be before he knew if they were intact.

After four days he was put in the main ward, where he hobbled up and down, carrying his drips with him. He asked for a phone, and contacted Trevor, his friend who had his work in his rucksack who said he would be round that evening. Jon asked him to find the newspaper printed the day after his attack and bring it for him to see.

Before Trevor arrived a nurse called to Jon telling him that a visitor was waiting to see him in the television room. Jon slowly staggered along the corridor, still swathed in tubes and bottles. Jon was puzzled for he did not know of anyone who knew he was in the hospital.

The visitor stood up, but did not offer his hand. "I'm from Special Branch. Sit down will you? I was in the crowd when you were attacked. I saw it all happening."

"Why didn't you stop it then?" Jon asked curtly. "After all the assailant made a dummy run at me to see if I had any minders."

"Had no chance," replied the officer drily. "He moved too fast, but we've got him in jail, and we were only waiting for you to die to charge him with murder."

"Whether you like it or not," retorted Jon, "I'll take jolly good care to see you don't have to do that."

"Glad you're so sure," came the reply, "but either way, whether you die or not, you won't be needed to give evidence, for the man has already pleaded guilty to assault. But," and here the officer paused, "but IF you recover, will you continue public speaking?"

"From the tone of your voice it would seem you'd prefer me to be dead. Typically callous of your lot. But what I am going to do is my own business, and none of yours. If that's all you want to find out from me, you've had a wasted journey. Goodbye." With as much dignity as he could muster, Jon gathered his tubes together, and crept back up the ward. He was exhausted with the effort and with the man's attitude.

Later that evening Trevor arrived. The young man and the older embraced silently, the effort of movement making Jon wince. "Well now, tell me all about it," Trevor asked. "But first here's the paper you wanted."

"Thanks, Trev," and silently Jon scanned the paper. He found what he was looking for, a statement saying 'there were no incidents in the Park on Sunday.'

"Look at that Trev, look at that. No bloody incidents. Here am I, nearly murdered, expected to die, and the event witnessed by a whole crowd of people, and corroborated by the Special Police, and the press report no incidents. Who is covering up and why is what I should like to know."

"Calm down, calm down," soothed Trevor. "Look, lets get out of here into that side ward. Got a beer in my bag. Thought you might like it."

Again Jon shuffled down the corridor. He still looked blue, and his hands and legs were cold. "You look a right state," Trevor said with a smile. "Just as soon as you're fit and well come to my place. Here's a spare key. I don't want any nonsense. A puff of wind would blow you over."

"You're worth a million, Trev, and I'll come as soon as I can get these tubes off me." Jon put the key in his pocket. The two talked long and hard, Trevor listening carefully. Between them they tried to analyse the attitude of the Special Police Officer, the mention of murder, and the lack of reportage of the incident by the daily paper. By the time the nurse came calling for the end of visiting hours Jon was tired out. He crept back to bed.

What a mess I'm in, weak as a kitten. Must get stronger. It's not quite a week since it all happened, but I must get stronger.

By the end of two weeks, all the tubes had been removed, all the stitches taken out. The surgeon came and sat on his bed and spoke to Jon in a fatherly way, though Jon was the older man. "Now, sir, you've had a narrow shave. You've lost all that blood, and your resistance to fatigue and sickness will be very low. I do advise you to take care of yourself. I understand you have somewhere to go, otherwise I would not let you out of the ward. Everything should heal nicely as long as you take care."

Overawed a little by the kindness of the man, Jon replied, "Thank you, doctor. If the world were made up of people like yourself we wouldn't be heading for disaster. But don't you worry, I have survived against enormous odds many times before this." The surgeon sat leisurely on the edge of the bed. "Go on, tell me about yourself," he said.

"You see," Jon continued, "I am fortunate enough to have this trust in the absoluteness of life and this trust sees me through the swings and roundabouts of the daily struggle. Don't think I am not grateful for your expertise and the care and attention of those around me here. Your knowledge has battled with the forces of evil and won. Soon it will be time for me to fight again with evil as I see it, and with my own weapons, ideas and words. Like you, who labour with the knife to battle with the enemy of life, we use words. It's harder, lonelier, but frighteningly powerful. One day, maybe, you'll understand all that I haven't been able to say."

The surgeon replied, "You're a remarkable man. But even the body of a remarkable man has its limitations. My advice to you is to acknowledge your humanity, that your heart and lungs and circulation have taken a knocking, and you need to be careful. I won't say more, as you probably won't listen." They both laughed. "But you must come to out-patients if anything untoward happens and ask for me personally. I will help you." With this the surgeon rose hurriedly, shook Jon by the hand, and left. Jon's eyes were moist, and he saw the glimpse of pain in the eyes of the professional.

That evening Jon discharged himself. He still looked blue, and had breathing problems, but his wounds were healthy though not healed. He collected his holdall and left the hospital, steeling himself to keep the tears away as he said his farewells to the nurses and doctors who had tended him. He tried to walk to Trevor's flat, but soon realised his limitations, and hailed a taxi. Trevor managed to keep him quiet for two days, but on the Sunday Jon was determined to re-visit the Park again. He took a bus, and found that even the high step up taxed his legs. Slowly he walked to Speaker's Corner. He was recognised immediately, and greeted warmly by those who had seen the attack. He was moved by their concern. He thought he would thank them all, and stood on a small box. But the effort was too great, and although he tried to project an appearance of self-confidence he had to apologise for his feeble attempts, but he promised to speak again when he was stronger. He walked slowly to the Park entrance, where after a rest on a seat he planned to catch a bus back to Trevor's flat.

Tired with his exertions Jon dropped into a light doze. When he woke he saw the silhouette of a man against the afternoon sun. It seemed familiar.

"Why bless me," he muttered when his eyes had become attuned. "If it isn't Sleeping Beauty himself. I certainly don't want to see you, and I'm sure you've got no reason to be looking for me." It was the Police Officer whose charge of assault had resulted in the spell in jail.

"It's you I'm looking for, right enough," the man snarled. "And I've a warrant here for your arrest." Jon's mind flashed back to his last court appearance.

It's that damned fine. I've forgotten all about the bloody thing.

Aloud he said, "And what's the charge this time?" He tried to appear nonchalant.
"You were found guilty of assault on a police officer, and the fine is outstanding. I must ask you to come with me to the Police Station." Sleeping Beauty was purring with victory.
"OK, I'll come with you. But you've got to go at my pace. If you'd had any sensitivity you'd see I'm far from well. But I shouldn't expect anything as civilized as that from you." Jon felt angry and his heart was thumping hard.

Take it easy, old cock, hold yourself in check. Got to ride this one out. Too much tension could easily knock me out. I was the one who used to stay cool at the Gestapo interrogations. Old Chalky just fainted. Mustn't do that, not now.

Another small crowd was gathering as Jon slowly levered himself off the seat, and with the officer clutching his arm, he moved to the nearby car. "There's no way you could fix a cock and bull story of assault with me in this state. I suppose I should count that as a blessing." Jon longed to goad this man, there was something unclean about his presence.
In the police station he was led to a small cell and left to wait. The hard chair hurt his buttocks, and his head swam. Soon Sleeping Beauty returned, followed by the Police officer who had called in at the hospital, and they led him down a long corridor into a Court Room.
By now Jon was passed caring of any outcome. The Magistrate tried to be understanding. He allowed Jon to sit down. "This will only be a formality," he explained

when he had read a summary of the charges. "If you agree to pay the fine and make a statement to that end, then you are free to go. We know you have money enough, and I advise you to finish with the matter. You are in no fit state for more legal proceedings."

Gruffly Jon said, "Give me the necessary forms, and let me get out. Talk about hitting a man when he is down. It's disgusting."

With a shaking hand he signed the documents and the cheque for the fine. "I'd like to know who gave you the authority to check my bank account. I'd like to know what you don't know about me. Precious little, it seems to me." Tired and ill, he tried to keep his dignity. "And now gentlemen, I presume I am free to leave."

Outside the police station Jon waited for a bus. Once aboard the bus he started to shake, first his teeth chattered, then his hands trembled, then the whole of his body vibrated with uncontrollable shudders. The route was familiar to him, but he had difficulty in picking out the landmarks.

Got to get back. Got to get to Trev's. Got to get out. Got to climb the steps. Got to find the door key. Got to open the door. Got to sit down.

Then the world went black, secondary shock had set in. When Trevor returned he found Jon bathed in sweat and urine, white faced with shallow breathing.

"My, you're in a state. How long have you been like this?" Trevor shook Jon who opened his eyes. "I'm going to phone the doctor. You're right bad."

"No, no doctor," Jon murmured. "Blankets, and a hot bottle. That's all. It'll pass. Just keep me warm. Sorry for being..." Jon faded out again. All that evening Trevor sat by the sofa, watching the sleeping man. With the warmth of the blankets and bottle, the shivering stopped but the sweating continued in streams. Not daring to offer Jon anything alcoholic Trevor passed water for him to drink, but he could only manage small sips. The night took a long time to pass. With the dawn peeping through the windows Jon took a hold on his life, his breathing became more regular and deeper, the sweating stopped, and he slept quietly. Trevor, ceasing his watchfulness, made himself coffee and laced it with brandy. He knew that Jon had ridden the tiger and won.

In the following days, Jon nursed himself back to strength. He was grateful to Trevor for the use of his home and made this clear, but Trevor wanted none of it.

"Just stop this living rough, is all that I ask," he said. "Find a place and settle down with your poetry and plays. You say yourself it doesn't take a wise man very long to prove himself a fool. This is just what you're doing. You speak into a void. The world that you speak about is the world that people dream about, but they realise it is only an illusion, the pounding mistakes of history have loaded the dice against that dream world. Why do you have to sleep rough? You tell me you seek to regain your integrity. That's very noble, but how stupid! Step back from that grey zone. What you are doing to yourself isn't right. You know you're welcome here for as long as you like, but I know you won't stay here because you think you'll be beholden to me."

"You're right there, Trev. When I'm a bit stronger, and sorted out my written stuff, then I'll be off again. You must understand that I'd rather be in the underground world than have an allegiance harnessed to a use that worked against the principles of life. I must go on doing what I'm doing until I feel that I can no longer serve this Supreme Intelligence that means so much to me. Be patient with me, Trev. One day, you never know, maybe my ideas and efforts will rub off on parts of humanity. Then my life will not have been worthless. But now, lets have a drink, and stop being serious for a moment."

"Point taken," replied Trevor, "and I promise I'll never reprove you again. We don't and won't need smoke signals or the telephone to understand each other. And whatever happens you'll always have my friendship."

The empty bottles littered the floor the next morning. Jon once more started to feel more like his usual hopeful self. He knew it was time to resume his journey. He knew he must sort out his writings and keep only that which was unique and credible. He knew he must discard the rest, millions and millions of words, words all jumbled and cluttered and not recordable. What he didn't know was whether he'd be strong enough to continue battle with the winter elements.

CHAPTER TWELVE

Bereft

During the next few weeks while the winter evenings were drawing in, Jon stayed quietly at Trevor's flat, trying to keep out of the way of the photographic equipment lying around in odd places. After his last poor effort at Speaker's Corner, he vowed he would not appear till he felt strong again and able to withstand the emotional and physical demands that public speaking put on him. But he was not idle. He made use of the time to scrutinize the work in the rucksack that he had left in Trevor's care.

I'll only keep what I can use, notes and facts for my speeches. And of course the finished poetry and plays. Took me ages that did, sometimes years. The rest's too untidy. Must have been mad to keep it, just scribbled words on any old bit of paper. I wrote what I felt and saw. Here goes. That's torn up now, memories of fucking Gloria in the churchyard. And here, ah me! That's my warning about the rain forests. Look at this, my ode to a new life, my daughter's. God, there's everything here that I've thought or felt, but no one else could understand it. I hope I'm right chucking it all into the basket. But I must travel light. Just going to have my one holdall with all the best stuff collected together. Don't want to have to rely on Trev any more. I love him as a friend, but he doesn't really understand what my ideals and ideas are for. Just got to keep this lot safe. Perhaps I'm a bit too suspicious of people's intentions when they see my holdall. It's so dirty and could easily hold a bomb. Maybe the ideas are a bomb, and that's what they want.

Six weeks after his injuries Jon found himself back outside, one leather holdall and a bundle of clothes in double plastic bags his sole possessions. His small bank account was nearly empty, the fine imposed by the Courts having been paid. He was dependent on his wits and his frail state of health.

His first project was to see Matilda and explain what had happened. Matilda's round face shone when Jon wheezed into her kitchen area.

"My goodness, man. What's you been doing? Worried mad we were. Heard you weren't coming back, but didn't know why. I miss you, man. I miss you." The familiar plate of sandwiches quickly appeared with a mug of tea. Jon sat on a tall stool and recounted his story as Matilda continued with her work.

"You look like a ghost," she flustered. "Wish you could come back. Got a new girl now. She's all the while a giggling. Pop and see me when you've time, and if that there holdall's trouble, leave it with me." Refreshed from that encounter Jon walked on down the side streets. His heart was pumping, and his breathing was very shallow.

I'm not as fit as I thought I was now I'm moving around. Got to play my cards carefully. Health won't stand too much of a shake-up. Hello, what's this? 'Help wanted, hours by arrangement.' Nothing ventured, nothing gained. This might just be the ticket for me.

He had seen a small advertisement in a bakery shop window. He went into the shop which had a counter along one side filled with rolls, buns and bread. There were no fancy cakes, just plain wholesome food. But the smell! He could feel the saliva in his mouth. Bread, glorious bread. He hitched himself onto a high stool and waited a moment.

"Vot can I do vor you?" a voice came from a side door, and following the voice came the baker, with tall white hat, white coat and floury hands.

"I need part time work, but I'm ready to do any hours

that suit you." Jon did not mention his injuries.

"Are you vell?" asked the baker looking suspiciously at Jon's face.

"I'm usually well, but I've had an accident. I want to get back to work as soon as I can. I can assure you I'll give good service, even if I am a little slow to start with."

"OK, let's huv a try," the baker replied. He was white haired, with bushy eye-brows slightly powdered with flour, and his face was creased with worry lines. When he smiled his eyes softened, but a guarded look quickly hooded any signs of emotion.

Looks as if you're a fugitive. Probably from a damned repressive regime. Seen that look before when I was on the run in Poland. People were afraid to let their feelings show, too dangerous when they didn't know who was friend or foe. Think I'm going to like him. God, I hope I can keep going. I'm dead beat already.

Jon was to work a moving shift of six hours out of the twenty-four. There was a tiny cupboard at the back of the premises where he could leave his holdall, and a toilet and basin for the use of the four other staff. Again his duties included washing up and cleaning the tables, as well as humping the heavy sacks of flour. Later he helped to knead the dough but the baker, and never anyone else, did all the measuring. It was hard and hot work.

After three hours on the first day Jon found sweat was pouring off his face. He was breathing fast. The baker looked at him anxiously.

"Vot iss the matter?" he asked. "Are you not vell?"

"I'm alright, really I am," Jon panted. "I won't let you down. It will be better tomorrow and better still the next day."

There were two coloured men on the shift, both well over six feet. They were the kindest gentlest men that Jon had met for several years. Together they nursed Jon through the first few days, lifting the heavier pieces of equipment for him and finding him a stool to sit on by the sink. Together they talked over mugs of tea and Jon heard of the difficulties they faced living in an alien land. Their aim in their lives was to earn enough money for their families to be comfortable while they were in a foreign country, and to save enough to send back to their own home. They were both intelligent and were working well below their capacities. Jon enjoyed working at the bakery and felt his limbs strengthening with the physical work, but he was still hampered by bad circulation and shallow breathing.

Cardboard Hall was inviting disaster to a man in his state, so he settled for Rolling Stock Hotel and tried to keep a low profile. This proved impossible for night after night he was hassled by the Railway Police to move on. Sleep, that most precious of commodities, was hard to get. The eternal tussle was on. The vagrants needed the warmth of the station concourses, the police had to keep the areas clear of begging, stealing and disruption of the flow of the travelling public. Violence on the vagrant was unnecessary, and when Jon saw glaring examples of this brutality on the homeless he decided to act to alleviate the continuing stress. He phoned the Railway Police headquarters and reported three separate incidents of violence where firm words and patience could have been used. The result of this conversation was a flea in his ear, and he was now known by name to the authorities.

Victoria Station six nights in a row. Shouldn't do it again, but I'm just too dead beat to go further afield. Know they will pick on me 'cos of reporting them. I know they've got to do their job, but why do they have to use violence? Here am I, open to violence from both the law and the unlawful. I suppose if I had to make a choice, I'd settle for violence from the law. Illegal violence leads to chaos... Ah, here's a good corner, well tucked away, and nobody else wanting it. Quite dark too. Hope they leave me alone.

He dropped into an uneasy sleep. Later he woke to find something cold and wet on his face. It was the muzzle of an Alsatian, a police dog on a chain.

"You come 'ere quick," said a coarse voice. "I've a bone to pick with yer. Knew we'd find yer some place. Damned cheek reporting me. Wot yer doin' 'ere?"

Jon straightened himself up slowly, cramped and stiff.

"Selling cloud space to prospective angels, and that doesn't include you. Now get off my back. There's real crime being committed all round here, and you waste your time accosting me."

"Put yer foot in it, and shut yer trap. You'll pay for reporting me. Good mind to set dog on yer. That 'ud larn yer a lesson."

Jon found himself in an arm-lock and was marched unceremoniously to the police station office. He was thrown into an empty room, and losing his balance fell on the floor. Too weak to get up quickly he was prey to the venom of the offended policeman and a mate who joined him. They kicked him savagely, head, ribs and legs. All he could do was to cover up.

With one final jab the policeman shouted, "that'll teach you not to report us again. Now get off that floor you bastard, and come with me." Slowly Jon struggled to his feet, and when charged with trespassing all his protests fell on deaf and unsympathetic ears. He was shoved out on to the street as the morning sun rose in the sky. Back at the bakery he was given tea and buns and sympathy, and soon felt less aggrieved, though his body ached from the beatings. That evening was pay-day, and the baker graciously commended Jon on the effort he had put into his first week's work.

Quite pleased with myself, I am. Legs have stood the strain. Breathing is still a problem, and I know I'm an awful blue colour still. Everything else seems in working order, but don't know about sex. Haven't had a shiver of an arousal yet, 'spose I've not seen the right bit of fluff. The old baker's a real aristocrat. Wonderful manners. Should like to have met him in his own country. More suited to running an estate than running a bakery. Now I'm off to get stoned. Done enough of self-discipline just to get well. Then I'll get myself together and start off at Speaker's Corner.

He walked slowly to The Rose and Thorn, where he was known and well liked. Drinks were swapped and talk was animated. Jon knew the company well enough to ask them to watch his holdall during his frequent visits to the outside toilets. Soon he was thoroughly pissed, care and need leaving his troubled soul. At closing time he staggered out into the night refusing the landlord's helpful offer to look after the holdall till the next day. The chill of the night entered his boozed frame, and in spite of his frequent visits to the toilet in the pub he tottered down the first alley-way to relieve himself again. He was watched by the law in a police car. They stopped Jon as he came out of the small mews.

"Excuse me, sir, what were you doing down that mews?" asked the sergeant.

"You know effing well what I was doing," retorted Jon. "If you live on the streets you have to piss on the streets."

"What have you got in your bag?" asked the sergeant.

"Not bombs, if that's what you think," replied Jon, his drunken state making him feel reckless. "And if you are going to charge me for something, do so. Even with a knuckle sandwich from you, a night at your expense is better than one on the streets."

"Would you please show us what's in your bag?" The sergeant was scrupulously polite.

"If you want to look inside, then do it yourself," and Jon dumped the bag at the sergeant's feet, who sifted through the papers and notebooks with care. He found nothing that interested him.

"That's OK, sir. Now don't let me find you somewhere

where you shouldn't be." The car sped away.

"Bloody fool," Jon called out. "Midnight in London, you show me somewhere where I should be."

Ruffled, angry and exhausted through fatigue and drink, he slept soundly in the passage of a shop doorway, making a pillow of his holdall. He was obscured from prying eyes by the heavy refuse boxes which the shop had discharged for collection. Awaking cold and sober the next morning he felt something was different. His first reaction was fear.

My holdall. Christ, where is it? It's gone. Someone must have nicked it while I was drunk. Damnation. Can't be a thief. Too many police around and they'd see someone carrying a heavy bag. Look too suspicious. Must be the law wanting to see into my thoughts. Do they think I'm a terrorist, or even inciting terrorism? Must get it back. Must report it's theft. God, this is worse than the attack on me. Why must I have all this just because I'm looking for honesty and justice?

He disregarded the heavy pumping of his heart as he went to the nearest police station. He stood by the desk, ignored for minutes by the constable. Eventually the constable looked up, saw Jon and the condition he was in, and showed his contempt. Jon knew he would get little support from such a man, but saw to it that the incident was recorded. All that day Jon prowled the streets, asking after his lost work in the nearby shops, asking the dustbin collectors, asking the foot patrol police, asking anyone he could. He was distraught and felt totally bereft. He did not know what to do next.

"Vot iss the matter wiv you?" asked the baker, when Jon turned up for his shift. "Haf you seen ghost? You haf not blue face today. You haf green face. Come. Haf some tea. Haf some roll and butter. Vot hass been done?"

"My work, my work in my holdall. It's been stolen. I'm sure it's the police. All the work of years gone in one night.

Sorry, governor, I'll pull myself together in a minute. Thanks for the tea. Won't let you down. Will start off..."

Jon didn't finish his sentence. His work mates crowded round him, eyes agog at his dilemma. Their concern and sympathy calmed him down enough to fulfil his duties, but his heart was leaden with despair. He had only his pad in his pocket left with a few of his most recent notes. Speeches in the Park would be more difficult without his back-up material.

When Jon left the warmth and camaraderie of the small bakery he walked towards St. James's Park. The air was still, heavy with brooding black clouds. He was neither hungry or thirsty. The baker had supplied more than he needed.

Think I'll doss down before the rain comes. Looks as if even the Gods are against me... Am I journeying on the right path? Does anybody understand me? Is all my speaking in the other Park doing any good? Damn it, this is the first time I've had any doubts at all about my purpose... Give yourself a kick in the pants and get on with it, old man. What's this? An enormous plastic sack. Perhaps my luck is turning... Now for a corner and some boxes.

He found a space he had not used before, tucked in between a mobile vendor's van, and the railings of a large house which was broken into flatlets. It was well before his usual bed time, but he settled down in his plastic bag which covered him from top to toe, and surrounded himself by an assortment of boxes. The sky cracked intermittently with thunder and lightening illuminating the fury of the night. The wind rose to a crescendo, rattling the vendors van, sheets of paper danced through the air. The storm broke with violence, water gushed all round him and into the drains. Without the plastic bag he would have been soaked, but tired beyond endurance, he suddenly and serenely lapsed into a peaceful sleep. The storm continued to rage, tiles dropped from nearby roofs, branches fell to the ground, but still he slept. When he woke he found the hood of the mobile van had landed inches away from his head. While he was straightening himself and his plastic bag three young people came down the steps from the flats. They were complaining of the noise of the storm, how frightened they felt, and how they couldn't sleep.

Well, well, well. A sleepless night for the three of them, well tucked up in a warm bed in a warm house. Here am I, sleeping like a baby in the open. What a cosmic joke!... And now after a cuppa, off to Speaker's Corner, see how the land lies, and then do my first speech after the blasted attack. Will gun for the IRA again, and snipe at the unions. Can do that without having to refer to my notes. I only feel half a man without my written work. Bloody police. I'm convinced it was them. Who else would want to read my stuff?

He approached Speaker's Corner slowly, trying to get the feel of the place again. He was instantly recognised. Sporadic hand clapping started and a pathway was made for him. The welcome made him feel both glad and humble. He found the attendant, and made the transaction for the stepladder as before. It was a strange feeling to mount the steps, waves of nausea swept over him as he remembered the attack.

He opened his speech by greeting the crowd, explaining the reason for his absence. He touched on the loss of his work.

"In spite of losing my holdall, which I am sure the police have taken, the thin blue line of law and order is an essential part of the fabric of our civilisation. They must be respected, but on their part they must not get corrupt. Law must be upheld. What goes on in Northern Ireland cannot be accepted. The crocodile tears they cry over their dead add up to hypocrisy. They should start crying for the unborn, and stop jumping around with guns. Guns, guns everywhere, with the finger on the trigger, and Hail Mary's going on over the coffins, crossing this way, crossing that way. It's the double cross they're suffering from. I accuse them of betraying the human race. OK, they can put me on the bleeding spikes, but they must stop this road to social suicide."

"Bravo, bravo," came calls from one side of the crowd. "Fuck off, we've had enough of you," came shouts from the opposite corner.

"I have one more thing to say, then I will stop. Out of the continuing disaster, one undeniable fact emerges. We are personally and collectively at the cross roads of history where the time fuse is set, and combustion is reaching proportions of alarm. Incisive action must be taken to establish the well being of all people and thereby create a diversion towards undreamed of goals of progress. If this fails to happen I fear for the future of humanity."

With these solemn words, Jon eased himself off the stepladder, and inched his way through the crowd refusing to answer questions. He was intolerably tired, aching in his limbs, with his chest burning. He realised he was nowhere as strong as he used to be, and viewed the remaining winter weeks with apprehension. He was not sure if he could survive in his present condition.

Chapter Thirteen

The Proposition

Through the cold winter months and on till Spring Jon managed to cling to life, his routine, his ideals and his tenacity. There were several moments when death through cold and fatigue seemed an inevitable outcome. He disciplined his thoughts away from pain and discomfort and managed to rise to the challenge of every day events. Sleep, that charmer when allowed to flow, soothed his troubles into acceptable proportions. Dirt was ingrained in his skin, and no amount of washing would scrub it away. Hot baths hurt his swollen feet, so he avoided those. The rash on his groin reappeared and started to fester. He tried hard to keep himself from smelling of stale sweat, the sweating bodies in the bakery was a fresh wholesome smell. He used the warmth of the ovens to rejuvenate his body, and he used the goodwill of his fellow workers to rejuvenate his spirit. He managed to keep away from conflict with the police, and his speeches in the Park were less inflammatory. They dwelled more on the conditions of the ever growing number of homeless, their despair, their squalor, the drugs and increasing crime. He was aghast at their suffering, but could do little to help. He knew he had to cruise through life till he regained his normal state of health.

One incident angered him. Resting after a stint at the bakery with a pint of stout, a small figure appeared at his table.

"Why blow me down, if it isn't Tucker. Now what are you up to? You look more wicked than ever. Haven't seen you for ages. Want me to do something?"

"That's ri', Guv. Gotta liddle job for yer. What abou'

it? Be'er are yer? Bad time on them spikes. Saw the lot, Oi did. Right mess, it was. Now, my liddle proposition's a bi' o' cake. Yer can drive, and yer go' bo'el." Tucker, the thief of the breakfast scenario, leered towards Jon.

The scheme that Tucker unfolded seemed realistic enough. The plan was for a hold-up to be staged the following day where the payroll of a large firm was to be snatched from their Headquarters.

"Yer can choose," Tucker said as if offering a gift. "Yer can 'old the gun, or drive bloody car. If yer 'old the gun yer 'ave to push lolly in suitcase. If yer drives yer 'ave to tie up the 'ead Clerk."

Jon began to stutter his dismay. But Tucker calmly tried to soothe his agitation by adding that the Head Clerk would offer no resistance as he too was in on the deal.

Then Tucker rose to go. "Can't wait. Got to plan it quick. Oi'll be back in an 'our to 'ear which yer want to do." He flicked a five pound note on the table. "Get yerself sumthin t'eat. Oi'll be back seven sharp." Jon sat rooted to the table, anger, dismay and surprise reddening his face.

Well, I'll be damned. The sheer audacity of him. Bet that fat man, Ben, who fixed the filming, is at the back of it. Here am I, suffering hardship to retain the integrity of my inner citadel, and I'm asked to rob with violence. Can't understand it. Just because I believe in values, and try to stick to them, I don't fit in this hardening materialistic world. Crime figures show trouble. Spiralling towards chaos, I'd say. I'm not going to touch that bloody money, and I'll be off before he comes back. Damn cheek.

Jon left the pub quickly, the money still on the table. In the evening paper of the following day he read that the proposition he had refused had been carried out successfully.

How gracious was Spring, laying out her flowers and hopes for all to share. Jon let the feel of new life flow through his bloodstream. He felt much fitter, his breathing was regular and he could climb stairs without stopping half way, his legs were as strong as ever, and the groin rash was drying out. He felt the time at the bakery had served its purpose. He had to explore new avenues and take up new challenges, encourage his fellow dosser. He would miss his coloured colleagues at the bakery, and he felt he was losing a friend when he shook hands with the master baker.

"Cum to see uss. Ve want you to cum to visit uss. It iss good to hear you talk. It iss liddle like 'ome. Vill you cum?" The baker pleaded for a promise.

"It is the season of the butterfly. It knows it has life, but it doesn't know the end of its journey. I'm like that. So I can't make promises."

"Understand, yess, understand. It iss good that way." The old man touched his forehead, turned and left the room.

With money in his pocket from a bonus, Jon decided he wanted a day on the downs at Epsom. He needed to feel clean air and smell fresh soil. He washed as well as he could, and put on his cleanest shirt. Sitting at a corner seat of the train, he watched the blossoms, the magnolias, the daffodils. He also watched a young girl on the opposite seat, her smooth face flushed, her eyes alight. She was dressed casually, and wore a look of innocence as if she were untouched by evil and lust. Her simple and trusting manner drove a dart through to Jon's heart.

Holy Moses. I'm complete. I'm not damaged. Bless you, dear girl, for making me sexually aware again. It's the first shiver of an arousal I've had since my injuries. Wouldn't harm a hair on your head, but thank you anyway.

With this silent acknowledgement to the girl, Jon realised how different she appeared to be from the youth of the underworld, where poverty, grime and cold were accompanied by cynicism and harsh expressions. At Epsom he walked slowly from the station up to the race course, and there he sat on a bale of straw, the sun enveloping him in its embrace. He took out his pad and let his thoughts flow towards the young girl.

```
Discover my child, what within you lies. Seek vehicles
of love, but do not pour compassion into bottomless
wells.  Seek rather the tranquil one who loves you
more than he loves himself.  Accumulate reserves of
well-being as a force to meet emergencies.  Let love
be freely given and daily replenished.  Let not error
turn love into a carnal weapon.  What you are now
is good, so continue to gladden the eye.  You graced
my presence for a moment, while you closely watched
the  passing  scene,  continue  to  grace  the  presence
of  others.   Be  open  in  your  mind to  accept  new
circumstances without anxiety.  May you cherish all
that you had within you before learning's envelopment.
It is your birthright to make incursions to the quiet
sanctity of your own self.  In this way God's grace
will,  like  the  rising  sun,  shine  in  more  revealing
ways.   Take  aboard  no  cargo  of  glitter  for  ports
at which you will never call, and make no rendezvous
that you cannot keep.  Be alone at times, but never
lonely,  for  in  silent  moments  you  will  find  out  who
you are.  May you understand the pull of Life force
and  meet  the  yardstick  of  excellence.
```

With a sigh Jon turned his attention to the sound of horses' hooves. Gorgeous sleek beasts were being led to the valley, aristocrats of their breed, they were servants to the greed and exploitation of man's need for gain. He walked slowly back to the station, somewhat heavy in heart, the thought of his constant efforts to fulfil his programme weighing heavily upon him. The train he caught was nearly full. Opposite him lolled an expensively dressed youth with his boots, dirty from lack of care, splayed on the seat in front.

"Would you mind if I asked you a question?" asked Jon of the youth in his most charming manner.

"Fire ahead," replied the youth confidently. "Ask anything you like. I'll tell you straight."

"From the cut of your clothes, and the gold ring on your finger you show obvious signs of culture." The other people in the carriage showed an interest in the dialogue. The youth smiled.

"Could you tell me," Jon continued, "why do you do now what I am sure you never do at home. Does your education that I guess your parents paid for teach you these manners? Just look at those boots making dirty marks where other people have to sit." The young man reddened as giggles and murmurs wove their way around the carriage. He straightened up trying to look unconcerned but said nothing.

It was imperative for Jon to find more work, and to keep the commitment to his public speaking resolute, without his writings he still felt exposed, like a crab without its shell. He recalled his time at the ITV studios, and how working in a big organisation suited his needs. Scanning the evening paper he saw an advertisement for a porter's job in the headquarters of a charity called Save Again. Once more he tidied himself up, and presented himself to the Personnel Manager. Once again the job of porter had not been filled, no one it appeared wanted to do menial work. Jon was offered the job, and he accepted it.

Seems a doddle. Longer day than usual, 9 - 4.30, but again I can get a subsidised meal. Got to collect the mail from the various branches and carry packages here and there. I'm at everybody's beck and call. Shan't like that much. If they go all la-di-dah, I'll soon put 'em right. Funny mixture of elderly women, and long haired ardent looking youths. Wonder how much money gets to the really poor, and how much is diverted on the way? P'raps I can find out. Knightsbridge is a good centre, even though it's on my Cardboard Hall beat. Mustn't let them find me. Maybe I can lay my hands on another outfit. My old friend Herbert across the river doesn't ring the changes, and he's not much left. Perhaps I'll find projects to talk about on Sundays. Must keep going, must have trust in my ability. Must let my inner consciousness guide me. It's so easily swamped by everyday trivia. I'm closer to Supreme Intelligence when

I'm alone, alone with the grass, the trees, the stars. Oh God, in whatever form you are, help me to maintain my strength of purpose.

The routine suited him, money for food and drink was sufficient, and he whipped himself to perform well at Speaker's Corner on Sundays. Most evenings he found himself in pubs in the side streets round Kensington and Knightsbridge. The liquid gun helped him through the long hours when he was unoccupied, unoccupied but open to get involved in any situation. Being stronger he now used Cardboard Hall as much as he could, for the station police were turning really nasty towards him. No one at Save Again knew that he slept outside. He often smiled to himself when he heard his fellow colleagues moaning about their living conditions.

After being paid double time for weekend work Jon went to a pub he knew well which sported a live band. It was near a hospital, so doctors and nurses nipped in and out between their duty hours. They seemed a happy crowd of people, save one young doctor. He sat alone, and Jon saw him wince when a popular tune was played. After a while the young doctor came over to Jon's bench.

"You're alone, and I'm alone. Let me buy you a drink," the young doctor said.

"That's mighty kind. I'll do the next one," replied Jon. When the drinks arrived, conversation started. The young doctor wanted to talk.

"I've been watching you from time to time when you come here," the doctor commented. "I'm sure you sleep out. Can tell from your skin. I don't know how you can stay so cheerful. I know you've known better days."

"Correct, on all points," replied Jon somewhat brusquely. "But don't let's waste drinking time by talking about the habits of an eccentric like myself. What's your problem? Sometimes you look as if you carry the world on your shoulders.

"I wish I could tell you."

"Come on, try," urged Jon. "It can't be worse than my life story."

Encouraged by Jon's willingness to listen, the doctor proceeded. "Alright, here goes. I'm the Registrar of two wards of people dying of cancer. They continually ask me if they can be cured, if they will live."

"What do you tell them?" asked Jon.

"I lie."

"How well do you lie? Convincingly, I hope."

"Very badly," admitted the doctor.

"Isn't it easier for them if they know they are going to die?" Jon ventured.

"For some, but for the young it's very hard. But some of the youngsters accept it courageously, it's a privilege to be with them. Their only thought is for their relatives."

"It seems a continual impasse for you," said Jon sympathetically. "I hope you have enough joy in your own life to compensate."

"The joy went out of my life when I lost my wife. She died of cancer too. I see death many times, and I'm still mourning my own loss. It's hard for me, there are so many questions I cannot answer. The threshold of pain, for instance, and how it varies. Life after death, the seemingly unfair allotment of tragedy. Why does God allow good people to suffer? I feel I ought to be able to help my patients more, and I can't answer all the questions. Time is so short for some of them. You can understand why I come here and drink."

Fleetingly the memory of his own family flashed through Jon's mind. "It's at times like this that I find words inadequate. One day, when the pain has lessened, you will find that life is for living. It seems at the moment you must live through your profession, helping your sick patients as well as you can. They don't really expect you to give them all the answers. Often they are calling for your attention, your time. In the silence of their own souls they probably know as much as you do. Remember, by just 'being' as you are, among all that pain and sorrow is a great form of silent bravery. But now, one more drink for the road."

The doctor smiled. "Thanks, I will, and thanks for those words. Now I'm soon off to a cosy flat, but I expect it's really the road for you. Not much sleep either coming your way."

"It's OK," Jon laughed. "Down the chute," and the drink burned his gullet. Later they both left the pub together, laughing and joking. Jon went looking for suitable sleeping quarters, this time in the Soho area, quieter at that time of night than the residential parts of town.

This looks just right to me. Office parking space, and nobody coming in to bother me. And plenty of boxes, and milk crates. Must be my lucky day. I'll have a quick pee then off to bed. Surely no one will see me. Could do with a long and uninterrupted sleep.

Jon chuckled to himself as he piled the flattened boxes on to the crates. He then slid inside two of the larger ones, and made a fence of the remaining few. He had just settled in when a car drew up at the entrance. There was no mistaking the ominous radio communication. It was obviously the Law, someone must have reported him. A tall figure banged the car door, and flourishing his warrant card he approached the pile of boxes.

"I'm a Police Superintendent," he said in a loud strident voice. "This is private property, and you're not allowed to sleep here. Get the hell out of here, or you'll be arrested." Then in a whisper he bent down and added, "You'll be nicked if you're here tomorrow. I'm just giving you the tip off. They only reason I'm telling you is that I prefer to catch thieves, and not make other peoples' misfortunes even greater. Now take the hint." In his official voice he said loudly, "And mind you see the bloody place is tidy when you leave it."

Jon fell into an instant and deep sleep. The next thing he knew was that dawn was breaking and he was being tipped off the milkcrates on to the ground by a uniformed heavy.

"Watcher name?" asked the constable.

"You bloody well know what my name is," replied Jon defiantly. He received a cuff round the ear.

"You tidy up those boxes," ordered the constable. Jon, fearing arrest, decided to play it cool and started to collect the boxes together. He took a look at the other uniformed man. It was the Police Superintendent of the previous night, a member of the law with understanding of the dosser's plight.

To Jon's surprise the Superintendent stepped forward. "You've five minutes to beat it." Shaken though he was it took him a good deal less than five minutes to get clear of the area. Trouble was to follow him a few days later. He had built up a passing acquaintance with the three youngsters who lived in the flats above the area of the vendors van, where Jon had slept during the storm. There was a tiny garden between the tall house and front wall, and the youngsters said Jon could sleep there when necessary. He found an enormous box and some corrugated paper. Well tucked into the box with the extra thickness beneath him, he pulled the phlanges across, and relaxed into the darkness. Soon he was in a deep sleep. Suddenly he was instantly awake, though he had heard no sound. He flung the phlanges open and there to his horror he saw three large dark figures peering into the box. He used the only weapon he had, his voice.

Loudly he shouted, "And who may you be? Do those buttons that I can see on your tunic really belong to the police uniform? You might be phonies for all I know."

"Just keep your voice down, we're police officers."

"Not bloody likely, I won't," Jon shouted. "I'm sleeping on private property, and the people upstairs know I'm here, and they'll soon know you're here too. If you are policemen where are your warrant cards?"

The three men rapidly disappeared into the night.

Bet they were ordinary criminals, feeding off suckers like myself. Thought I was a soft touch. I'm too jittery and wide awake to stay here, in spite of my lovely warm box. God, how I needed that sleep. My whole body yearned for it. Must off to Covent Garden now for a cuppa. Come on, old man, don't get sorry for yourself. Those stars look friendly enough, and the air is soft. Feel more myself when I've had a cuppa. Come on, legs, get a move on.

Chapter 14

Ace of Spades

Jon worked through the summer at Save Again. It was an inefficient organization with over zealous people climbing over each other to claim funds for specific projects. Orderliness was non-existent, pounds could be saved with pruning unnecessary expenditure. Jon's temper flared when he was expected to be in two different places at once, and was unable to justify his movements. Lowly though his position was he resented the off-hand way he was addressed by people half his age, and he made this point clear. Sometimes he wondered why he was where he was, and whether this humdrum routine was stifling his creative thought. Sometimes he was late for work, he was either too drunk, too stiff and cold or had been too involved with night time sessions with his fellow dossers under Waterloo Bridge. He would wash himself down, juggle with what clean clothes he had, and appear with a grin at the Porter's desk. The Head Porter was a sympathetic man, who was very easy going and never made a fuss.

"You're not as bad as some of these modern fellows, jerseys, jeans and long hair. It's the old army of old ladies who come to do their voluntary bit that puts us all to shame. Back-bone of the country they are. Now, young man," the porter winked at Jon, "you've got a stint at the post room today. Mind you get the stamp machine working properly or we'll all be in a fix. Had breakfast yet? You look all dishevelled. Best go quick and have a cuppa. Bad as the youngsters you are, coming to work without a proper breakfast. Not good for you. I always have my breakfast. My Mary gives me a whopper." Jon turned away, leaving the cheerful man talking to himself. He went to the canteen and had a quick cuppa, felt better immediately, and was able to approach the post room work with equanimity. He survived the pressure for the first day, letters here, parcels there, airmail, registered, weighing this, bagging that. He was not used to being pressurised with such detail. After work he left the building, and found a bench in a small park. He let his mind empty of hassle and wrote in his pad.

Here I am, moving swiftly to my terminal point in life, and I wonder at my situation. I'm at the beck and call of people whose minds are too full of trivia to be inspired by truth. They seek to enhance living conditions in physical and practical ways. They do not seek the journey to soul, the journey to soul being the purpose of MY life, the journey to my own soul and to help others find their way to this end. I am a square peg in a round hole, and although there are hours aplenty for my own thought, I feel my purpose to help humanity steer clear of this oncoming abyss is fraught with negativity. My efforts with the dossers is only transient, the suffering and loss of dignity blunts the memory of my words. My speeches in the park seem to fall on deaf ears. I appeal to you, God, the consciousness of the world, the Supreme Intelligence, who has succoured me through my life, don't let me feel bereft of your presence. Is it Your will that I stay on this path that I followed these last years, or should I try another way? Should I use my pen alone to advocate change? My instincts tell me that I should not persevere with what I am doing now, personally and verbally supporting the underdog, decrying evil and challenging the unnecessary power of some establishments. The odds are too great against me. Just one against all those who have no integrity. Should I try to spread my thoughts and ideas through the written word?
In which direction I should go I must leave the force of Life, through You, to direct me.

Jon read the words slowly.

Goodness me, I have let my morale get low. What are those words I wrote in the prison camp? Let not your mood be lowered by that grim wind outside, for that same force will ripen tomorrow's corn to feed man's body first, and then perhaps his soul. Will the wind of materialism and corruption and untruths ever feed my soul?... Never... I must find the wind of Life, come what may. That'll feed my soul. But to the moment of 'now', and that moment is to escape. That shows the frailty of my nature. John Barleycorn and a few hours oblivion. Here goes!

True to his intentions Jon did just that. He bent he elbow as many times as he could during the course of the evening. At closing time he tottered out of the pub doorway and into the street. He didn't pay attention to the police car parked nearby. Peeing frequently as he moved, he at last found an alley way, which was stacked with plastic bags on one side waiting for the rubbish collector. Lurching into this alley way he fell fast asleep, not bothering to find boxes or plastic bags for himself. As dawn appeared he regained reasonable sobriety. Then he heard the dust cart.

Hell, I must get a move on or I'll be swept up with the rubbish. Have a quick stretch. That's better. God Almighty, whatever's this? My holdall. My damned holdall. Thought I saw a police car last night but didn't take any notice of it. They must have followed me, and dumped it here when I was blotto. Now, is everything here? Yes, yes, there's the play. And the poems. And look, even the handtowels and my poignant scribbles. Wonder why they kept it so long? Wonder what the hell is going on? Probably photo'd every page of it. Stupid suckers, they should've known I wasn't against the realm. Perhaps this is a signal to point the way I have to go. Maybe this is the way the forces of Life are showing me to persevere with my pen and not my tongue. It's all so wonderful, so real.

"Watch it, mate, or you'll finish up in the cart." A burly dust-cart man came hustling towards the alley.

"O.K., bud, I'm off. Found a lot of us, have you? Must make it a bit hard for you, poking up the human bundles."

"It's alright mate. It's alright. Kind 'uv get used to't. Can't do nuffink 'bout it. Too much effin' poor and too much effin' rich, that's wot I say." He strode off with four plastic bags draped around him.

Jon was on his fifth cup of tea before he could accept the enormity of the treasure before him, the old familiar holdall. He felt in the land of the living again. He went to work in the post room with a light heart, new life seemed around the corner.

"You here again? You look more cheerful than yesterday. Something nice happened?" A silver haired, tall and angular woman loaded with a pile of parcels to post peered round her parcels and smiled. Her keen blue eyes, wrinkled at the edges, looked directly at him. "Yesterday, it seemed as if it were all too much for you, I was a bit anxious."

"Today's fine, just fine. Better than yesterday. My name's Jon. You probably know that already," he smiled quizzically, peering through his pebble glasses that he needed for close work. "Seen you a bit, but don't know where you fit in."

"They call me Helena here," she replied, "but my name at home is Betty. I fit in alright. Got to. It's my job. Look, I've a whole lot more packets to bring you. This happens once a month. My army of old lady volunteers do the whole job. Regular news letter. Stupid waste of time and money, but I daren't say so."

"Keeping me out of mischief are you, Helena. Your blue eyes are twinkling alright." Jon was laughing too. "Could we meet for a cuppa in the lunch hour - that is if you've no one else you're meeting?"

"Bit bold, aren't you?" she quipped. "No, there's no one else." Her eyes clouded over and Jon with his sharp perception muttered under his breath, "Something hurting, is it?" She pretended not to hear the care in his voice, and said cheerfully. "OK, 1.45, top canteen for a cup of tea. That'll be fine."

That was the beginning of change. She was tall silver-haired and angular and very soberly dressed so they made an odd couple, Jon wearing his mis-matched clothes. They met frequently in the canteen and talked and talked. Instantly they felt their souls were in tune. Jon asked Helena about herself, and she, in her hesitant and jumbled way replied as honestly as she could. Helena was fifty and was trying to remould a life after a broken marriage, and her self-esteem was very low. From the psychological blows she had received she found it difficult to trust. This led to the hesitancy. Jon listened carefully, encouragingly. Helena found him both soothing and stimulating and she looked forward to the next meeting and the next. She had no idea of his background, his aspirations or his present mode of living but she could feel he had been through periods of great suffering.

One day, the following week, Helena found a bunch of red roses on her desk. With them was a letter. It said, "This gift of roses is for you, in acknowledgement to the gracious way you have led your life. I notice your outward lookingness, your non-fashionable sense of honour and your clarity of mind. You are indeed a beautiful lady and worthy of a bowl full of flowers on every day of your quiet heroic existence. From your friend (and admirer), Jon."

Helena was confused, but delighted, for it was a long time since she had been made aware of her femininity. This bunch of roses led to a great deal of talking and understanding. They wandered slowly along paths of togetherness. All she knew was that she had never been loved before for what she really was, warts and all; she had only been loved for an image, an image she never could become. She was beginning to learn of Jon's stony path of life, and her heart bled for him. Her story seemed mild and uneventful, but Jon listened intently when she talked.

One day, walking hand in hand through dapple lit woods, Jon stopped.

"Helena, my love, I want you to take this back with you to read when you are on your own. Although I am a great talker at most times, I find it hard to express my deep inner feelings about you, to you. From our talks together over these last weeks we both know we are drawn towards each other, perhaps irrevocably. Here, here, take this. I wrote it last night by the light of the moon." Pushing a creased piece of paper which he had torn from his notebook into her hands, he blushed like a first time lover.

When she arrived back at her tiny home she drew the curtains and read his words.

Helena, life has dealt me out the Ace of Spades, **you**, the trump card in the pack, and I am truly fortunate. Allow me to play the hand in humility, but with honesty. When the safety of the conventional codes are forsaken, and the brakes of repression are eased, more self discipline is needed in the control of the new found and powerful emotions which are driving me dangerously. While the road from our different pasts which brought us together has had so many separate hurts, we will be able, through love, to charter a new history together. But these roads made us what we are becoming to each other. Any disharmony from our former separate selfs we will replace with love, and we will live where only **now** is present. If anything in the world that only lovers know is sacred, it is in the growth and harmony of two people searching for the strength for life to begin.

Oh, Helena, will I be worthy of your loving overtures? Your break for selfhood had begun long before I appeared, and although you're still trapped in many loyalties you seem able to toss aside security and dependency and be free of orthodoxy's suffocation. From our two opposite worlds we will find a unity of purpose on which to build.

What compensation can I give to you if you share your life with someone who is still under the influence of the 'outside', with nothing to offer but love?

I've no settled future, no bank account, no prospects. I will work with my pen though I do not know that outcome. But I have hope, I have a deepened sense of consciousness and I have my manhood, and I know I am sexually complete again after the attack in the Park.

These words and the sense of urgency and purpose that Jon surrounded Helena with were bewildering. She lived alone in a terraced city house, eking out her small income to the best of her ability. She had to reason long and hard. There she was, a conformative, middle class divorcee, working at Save Again to earn a living. She had no sense of poetry, and had never entered the world of pubs, horses, or freedom of speech that Jon spoke of so frequently. Would she put a curb on this extraordinary man who had come into her life, she wondered. Would her respectability hinder his free flow of movement and thought and dampen his original thinking? Would he be content with what she had to offer, a daily pattern, regular food, but very little money? Anxiety gnawed at her vitals, making the nights devoid of sleep. She wanted the excitement and stimulation that he offered her inner being, she wanted to be led into new and wider areas of thought, and she wanted to enjoy the many likes in common, nature, music, laughter. And after many arid years of abstinence she yearned for the sexual awareness he was arousing in her.

She felt free enough to put all these anxieties before Jon. "But I've thought of all that," he replied, "I've even thought of how I'll feel if I can't make enough money to support you. But I feel so strongly that Life has given us this opportunity to grasp a new start of knowing we would be foolish to turn away.

After weeks of meetings in public places, and lying together talking in the parks, declaring their love but still not able to make their bid for togetherness, Helena made a suggestion. "Jon, darling. Would you ever feel you could manage to live in my house? I could do the typing for all your written work, and we could market it together. It would be a new way for you to work, your thoughts may be able to flow more freely without the hassles of living rough. I would try to give you all the emotional space you needed, and you would be free to go if and when you wished. God forbid." She paused, waiting for a comment from Jon, but none came. "It would make me very happy if you chose to come. This could be a real new beginning for us both." She paused, hesitant. "I've got a suggestion," she continued slowly, "tomorrow, walk up the road carrying all your luggage. I know it's not much, 'cos I've seen it." She laughed a little nervously. "If you have your luggage with you, I will know you've come to stay. If you come just by yourself, I know you have decided to continue with your own way of life, and I won't mention it again."

Jon said nothing, but picked a buttercup and handed it to her.

All the morning of the next day Helena dithered round the house, as anxious and excited as a young girl. She kept watching the road, screwing her eyes against the sun. There, at last, she saw him. He was carrying all his luggage, his one piece, his holdall. He was coming to stay.

They were together until he died, working away, working away.

Return from Despair

I met a woman when I was on my way
Though all around me was amid decay
And on reason's clinging ledge
Was little salvaged, naught to dredge
For I had by-passed hope, yet all
Was not lost or won or was impossible.
Swiftly unseen the impossible became real,
The only limits were those placed by me,
She helped me to return to reality.